how to raise an
AMAZING
CHILD

the Montessori way to bring
up caring, confident children

TIM SELDIN
President of the
Montessori Foundation

DK

LONDON, NEW YORK, MUNICH,
MELBOURNE, DELHI

Senior editor Esther Ripley
Senior art editor Glenda Fisher
Project art editor Sara Kimmins
Project editor Angela Baynham
Designer Hannah Moore
Photographer Vanessa Davies
DTP designer Sonia Charbonnier
Production controller Mandy Inness
Managing editor Penny Warren
Managing art editor Marianne Markham
Picture researcher Carlo Ortu
Jacket designer Glenda Fisher
Jacket editor Adam Powley
Publishing director Corinne Roberts

The ideas and methods used in this book are based on
the author's experience as a Montessori teacher and
parent and on the lives and experiences of the many
families he has been associated with. While Montessori's
ideas have been used successfully in school and at home
with generations of children, readers should use their
own good judgment in deciding which to adopt or
carry out in their own family. Neither the author nor
the publisher shall be liable or responsible for any loss
or damage allegedly arising from any information or
suggestion in this book.

First published in Great Britain in 2007 by
Dorling Kindersley, A Penguin Company
80 Strand, London, WC2R 0RL

A CIP catalogue record for this book is available
from the British Library

ISBN 978-1-4053-1299-8
Reproduced by Colourscan, Singapore
Printed and bound by Tien Wah Press in Singapore

See our complete catalogue at
www.dk.com

contents

introduction

I can't remember a time when I wasn't involved in the world of Montessori — for me it is a way of life.

This book is a compilation of my personal experience as a young child, as a father, as a Montessori guide and as something of a coach to many families who have sought a better way to raise their children in a spirit of kindness, partnership and respect. Much of what I have learnt came from observing and listening to my children and from my mistakes.

Being a parent is a full-time job. Once upon a time, raising a family seemed straightforward. Mums stayed at home and looked after the children, while dads went out to work. Children were generally obedient, if only because their parents punished them severely if they were not.

Today, things are different. In many families, mum is not at home all day. She may have a career or business or she may have to work just to make ends meet. Young children are often cared for in nurseries or in the home of another woman who earns her living by looking after a small group of children too young to go to school. In many countries divorce has become quite common, and many mothers, and some fathers, juggle the responsibilities of work and parenting in a single-parent household.

Meanwhile, stories in the newspapers, magazines and on TV report recent findings showing how important the right environment and experiences are for babies, toddlers and young children. We understand that children's brains are programmed to learn, but only if they are stimulated at an early age. As if we didn't have enough guilt before, now we get to worry about whether we are good enough as early childhood parent-educators.

Most of us long to give our children the best home environment that we possibly can, within the limits of our time and resources. If you have a young child at home and are eager for a fresh perspective and some practical suggestions, then this book is for you! While not every teacher is a parent, every parent is a teacher. The mission that we've undertaken is not simply to feed, cuddle and protect our children. We will also need to teach them to become independent, self-confident, successful adults, who are happy and fulfilled in their lives. While that journey takes many years, it helps to have some idea of where you are heading and why we do what we do along the way.

I hope this book will encourage you to enjoy your time with your child more than ever. It is filled not only with ideas for activities to do together, but with a message that life can be celebrated. The small everyday things that we can do to mark special occasions and to reaffirm our love for one another can make all the difference in the world, both for your child, and for your own life as a mum or dad.

Tim Seldin

Tim Seldin
President, The Montessori Foundation

"while not every teacher is a parent, every parent is a teacher"

CHAPTER
ONE

why
Montessori?

the highs and lows
of parenting

Children are one of life's greatest gifts – but raising caring, happy children in this modern world can be a challenge to any parent.

A bond for life From the moment they are born, our children become the most significant focus of our lives.

Our connection with our children is formed before birth, and lasts for our entire lives. Over the years, we are there beside them as they learn to smile, crawl, speak their first words, take their first steps, and together we mark the milestones in their journey towards adulthood.

Life with children is not always easy. Sometimes, along with the hugs and cuddles, we share their sleepless nights, the times when they are ill, their temper tantrums and fights with siblings and the many other challenges of being a parent. As they get older, it seems that our children come to know us better than we know ourselves. They learn what buttons to push to make us aggravated and how they can best manipulate us into giving in over something that they want. There are times when we wish our children came with a parenting manual.

It's not unusual for parents to be unsure about how to raise nice kids in this modern world. All around, our children see and hear other children answering back to their parents, arguing in the playground and saying unkind things to one another. Parenting advice abounds, but much of it doesn't seem to work that well. This is in part because it tends to offer a cookbook approach with detailed suggestions about what to do in specific situations, rather than a comprehensive, systematic approach to parenting.

a different approach

My life has been touched deeply by the work of a brilliant woman: Maria Montessori. As a child, I went to a wonderful school that was inspired by her work and as an adult I have had the privilege to teach in and later lead that same school for 25 years. Her message and the insights and practical strategies that she taught have influenced hundreds of thousands, if not millions, of parents and children around the world. The Montessori approach is best known in the schools that bear her name, but it is equally useful and easy to adopt in your home.

Montessori's principles for working with children are based on a holistic approach that begins at birth (or as young as possible) and builds over the years as children become more mature. Understood correctly, it has the advantage of working very well with a wide range of children. It is an entire system that has been tested over the past 100 years and can be implemented as a whole or in part. Try it – you should find that it works for you, too!

On the run As children grow, the challenges of parenthood are demanding but rewarding.

To do this, you don't need to become a Montessori teacher, nor is there a need to create a Montessori school in your home. But by implementing as many of the suggestions in this book as you can into your home and your family's life, I believe that you will find yourself becoming more effective as a parent, and more able to build a home filled with warmth, love, kindness and respect.

what is
Montessori?

One hundred years ago a young Italian woman devised a new approach to education based on a foundation of encouragement and respect.

Maria Montessori was born in 1870 in Italy, a country that at that time was especially conservative in its attitude towards women. Despite many obstacles, Montessori was the first Italian woman to become a doctor. She went on to teach at the medical school of the University of Rome, and, through its free clinics, came into frequent contact with the children of the poor. Through her work she became convinced that all children are born with an amazing human potential, which can develop only if adults provide them with the right stimulation during the first few years of life.

Anxious to prove her point, in 1907 Montessori started to oversee a nursery for working-class children who were too young to go to school. Located in one of Rome's worst slums, this became her first Casa dei Bambini or "children's house". The conditions were appalling, and many of the children who entered were aggressive, impatient and disorderly.

Montessori began her work by teaching the older children how to help out with everyday tasks. To her amazement, three and four year olds took great delight in learning practical living skills. Soon these children were taking care of the school, assisting with the preparation and serving of meals and helping to maintain a spotless environment. Their behaviour changed from that of street urchins running wild to models of grace and courtesy.

a child's world Montessori recognized that little children experience a sense of frustration in an adult-sized world, so she had miniature jugs and bowls prepared, and found knives that fitted into a child's tiny hand. She had carpenters build child-sized tables and chairs that were light enough for children to move without adult help. The children loved to sit on the floor, so she gave them little rugs to define their work areas and they quickly learned to walk around them rather than disrupt each other's work.

After spending countless hours observing and interacting with children, Montessori concluded that they pass through several developmental stages (see pages 14–17), each one characterized by specific inclinations, interests and ways of thinking. She found that children have their own logic at each stage of development, along with certain preferred activities and natural tendencies in behaviour.

She observed how children respond to a calm and orderly environment in which everything has its allocated place. She watched the children learn to control their movements, and noted their dislike of the way the calm was disturbed when they stumbled or dropped something. She gave them the opportunity to develop their sense of independence and recognized their increasing levels of self-respect and confidence as they were taught and encouraged to do things for themselves.

A new beginning Italian doctor Maria Montessori founded a new approach to educating children.

international appeal The first children's house received instant acclaim and interest surged around the world. As an internationally respected scientist, Montessori had a rare credibility and she captured the interest of national leaders and scientists, labour leaders and factory owners, teachers and mothers. She gave up her medical practice to devote her energy to overseeing the spread of Montessori schools around the world. A tireless advocate for the rights and intellectual potential of all children, she continued her research until her death in 1952.

Montessori's work lives on today. Her systematic approach can be replicated and sustained in almost any situation. Some people are attracted to the calm, responsible behaviour shown by these students, and appreciate their love for learning. Others applaud the freedom, spontaneity and independence that Montessori gives young children.

KEY
IDEA

sensitive periods
for learning

Children pass through "sensitive periods" in which they are primed to learn, and some of these opportunities don't come twice.

"during a sensitive period children become intrigued by aspects of their environment"

Montessori recognized that children go through stages of intellectual interest and curiosity – which she called "sensitive periods" – in which they become intrigued and absorbed by particular aspects of their environment. It is important that we understand this process because each stage represents an opportunity which, if taken advantage of, can profoundly influence our children's development.

Montessori identified several different sensitive periods occurring from birth through to age six (see pages 16–17). Each one refers to a predisposition compelling children to acquire specific characteristics. For example, during the first few years of life, children are in a sensitive period for language. They pay close attention to what we say and how we say it, and before we know it they speak the same language as us and with a similar accent.

When parents and teachers recognize and take advantage of the sensitive periods through which children pass, they can become more effective in supporting their learning and development.

Each sensitive period is a specific kind of compulsion, motivating young children to focus intently on some particular aspect of their environment, day after day, without becoming tired or bored. Clearly, this is a biological mechanism hard-wired into children, that helps them to

develop skills and talents that are inherently part of our heritage as human beings. Inevitably, the beginning and end of each sensitive period will often differ from child to child, so we need to watch carefully and respond to our children individually. Remember that your child's learning during these early stages is the foundation upon which much that follows will be built.

A time to learn Given the right stimulation at the right time, children are able to learn almost unconsciously.

limited opportunity During a sensitive period, children can learn new things, master new skills or develop aspects of their brain's abilities painlessly and almost unconsciously. However, sensitive periods are transitory states. Once children have mastered the skill or concept in which they were absorbed, the sensitive period seems to disappear, so if children are not exposed to the right experience and stimulation at the right time the opportunity to learn will pass. The skills can still be learnt, but now it requires years of hard work and drill. This is why, for example, learning one or more languages is relatively easy for children at the age of two and three when they are in a sensitive period for language, but much more difficult for most of us as adults.

sensitive periods (birth to six years)

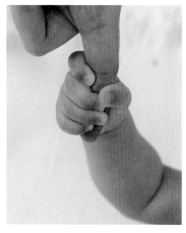

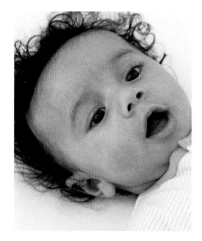

Movement (from birth to one year) Your baby's random movements become coordinated and controlled as he learns to grasp, touch, turn, balance, crawl and walk.

Language (from birth to six years) Starting with practice coos and sounds, your baby progresses from babble to words, phrases, then sentences.

Small objects (from one to four years) Your child will adore small objects and tiny details as hand-eye coordination becomes increasingly refined and accurate.

Order (from two to four years) Everything must have its place. This stage is characterized by your child's passionate love of routines and a desire for consistency and repetition.

Music (from two to six years) When music is part of his everyday life, your child will show spontaneous interest in the development of pitch, rhythm and melody.

Toilet training (from 18 months to three years) As her nervous system becomes better developed and integrated, your child will learn to control her bladder and bowels.

Grace and courtesy (from two to six years) Your child will love to imitate polite and considerate behaviour leading to an internalization of these qualities into her personality.

Senses (from two to six years) Sensory education begins at birth, but from two your child will be fascinated with sensorial experiences (taste, sound, touch and smell).

Writing (from three to four years) Montessori discovered that writing precedes reading and begins with attempts to reproduce letters and numbers with a pencil and paper.

Reading (from three to five years) Children show a spontaneous interest in symbols and the sounds they represent – soon they are sounding out words.

Spatial relationships (from four to six years) As your child develops an understanding of spatial relationships, he becomes increasingly able to work out complex puzzles.

Mathematics (from four to six years) Montessori found ways to give children a concrete experience of maths in the period of sensitivity for numbers and quantities.

ACTIVITY
FOCUS

the magic of Montessori
schools

The Montessori message is just as meaningful today and is thriving in schools around the world.

Children who are treated with respect and who are encouraged to try new skills learn more readily to do things for themselves. Montessori taught that a child who feels respected and competent will develop a far greater level of emotional well-being than a child who is simply loved and doted upon.

Montessori teachers share a conviction that success in school is directly tied to the degree to which children believe they are capable, independent human beings. Young children are shown how to pour liquids, write letters and compute sums. Older children are shown research techniques, internet search routines and more advanced forms of writing. When children develop a meaningful degree of independence, they set a pattern for a lifetime of good work habits, self-discipline and a sense of responsibility.

freedom to learn
In a Montessori classroom there are some basic ground rules about behaviour and tidiness, but beyond these children are free to choose whatever activity they wish, and to work with it for as long as they want to. They are free to move about and work alone or with others at will. Much of the time children select work that captures their interest, although teachers help them to choose activities that will present

Getting ready to work When working on the floor children mark out their work area with a small mat.

Neat and tidy The Montessori classroom creates a sense of order that encourages children to become self-disciplined and independent.

new challenges and new areas of inquiry. When they are finished with an activity, children are expected to put the materials back where they belong. Students are taught to manage their own community, and they develop independence and strong leadership skills.

Such guidelines easily adapt to the home. If you create a welcoming but orderly space for your children and allow them to work and play freely, their confidence and independence will blossom.

BUTTONING UP Practising on a dressing frame helps children master the skills needed to dress themselves.

SHOE POLISHING Children love to polish brass and silver, then move on to polishing their own shoes.

LEARNING TO POUR Small jugs just right for children's hands are used to teach them how to pour.

LEARNING LETTERS Children learn to read phonetically. They compose words and sentences using the "Movable Alphabet".

HANDWRITING To help develop the hand-eye coordination needed to correctly grasp and write with a pencil, children trace shapes onto paper.

SENSORIAL EQUIPMENT These wooden cylinders, graded in size and depth, help children to explore and refine their senses.

right from
the beginning

Babies are born curious, creative and intelligent. Alongside basic baby care, enrich your child's world to help him achieve his full potential.

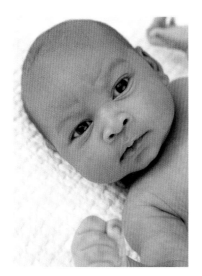

Absorbent minds From the moment they are born, children are responsive and receptive to all aspects of their environment.

While babies are different from adults in many important ways, each is a full and complete human being who is present in the room with us, absorbing every sight, sound, smell and touch that he experiences into his deepest memories. When, as parents, we truly understand this, we can become more aware of the impression left by what we do, what we say and what we allow our children to come into contact with from the moment of their birth and through the first days, months and years of their lives.

a gentle birth There was a time, not so many years ago, when babies were delivered in hospital operating rooms. After nine months floating in the warm, cosy, dark environment of their mother's womb, experiencing only muffled sounds, babies went through the trauma of birth and entered a brightly lit, noisy room where the air was cool, and where they were handled roughly. It seems difficult now to imagine a newborn being held by a leg as the doctor gave it a swat on its bottom to get it breathing, yet this used to be common practice. Next, rather than allowing mother and baby to meet one another and rest, the umbilical cord was swiftly cut and the baby was taken off into another room to be weighed and washed.

A wonderful journey Every physical milestone your baby achieves is driven by the need to experience more.

"babies are full and complete human beings…absorbing every sight, sound, smell and touch that they experience"

Today, thanks in part to Montessori's influence, more compassionate health care professionals assist in the process of birth. Modern birthing centres and hospitals use subdued lighting; the room temperature is kept warm, soothing music can be played and everyone speaks in hushed voices. After the birth, the newborn is placed on the mother's tummy to rest and bond before being washed off, weighed and checked over. Except in rare medical emergencies, everything is handled at a relaxed pace.

bonding with your newborn In the first few hours after birth, there is a sensitive period in which infants form a particularly close bond with their parents. According to Dr Silvana Montanaro, from the Association Montessori Internationale (AMI) Assistants to Infancy centre in Rome, "Research has shown that the extent and quality of care the mother provides the child are strongly conditioned by the way they spend their time together during the first days after birth."

"In the first few hours after birth, there is a sensitive period in which infants form a particularly close bond with their parents."

This connection begins from the physical contact experienced as the baby is cuddled and touched by his parents, and quickly becomes the emotional connection that we celebrate in all healthy relationships between parents and children. It is a two-way connection. The baby feels safe in his parents' arms, and forms a powerful and lasting impression of their faces, smell and the sound of their voices; at the same time, the parents usually fall head over heels in love with their child, which goes a long way to helping them keep going in the early months when they are deprived of sleep and adjusting to new parenthood.

Both parents should take turns holding and caressing their newborn, to ensure a close bond is formed with each of them. Gently stroke your baby while he lies in your lap or hold him against your bare chest to establish the warmth of skin-to-skin contact.

Almost all babies, and in particular those who are born prematurely or who face medical challenges, respond beautifully to gentle infant massage. Massage relaxes your baby and deepens the bonding process. It is also known to contribute to restful sleep and good digestion. There are many books and videos available that demonstrate and explain how to massage your baby.

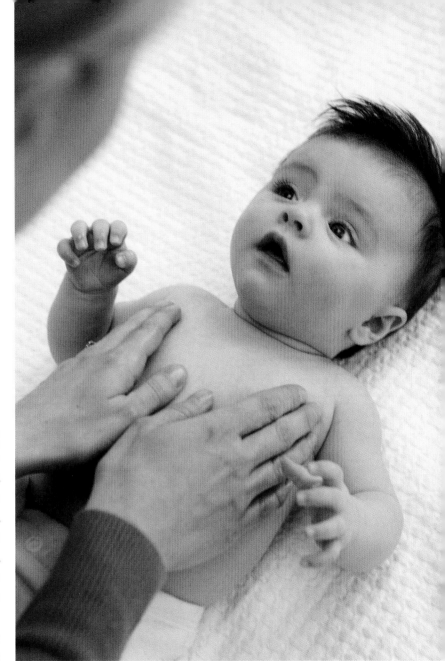

soothing and settling

Babies enjoy the sounds of baby talk from adults: cooing, singing, talking in silly voices all tend to hold their attention. And of course, it is universally acknowledged that reciting poetry or nursery rhymes, singing lullabies or reading aloud as you gently rock in a chair are the best ways to soothe a crying baby.

Some babies startle and cry easily, while others find it difficult to fall asleep or they may be unusually sensitive to touch, light or sound. Don't be alarmed if your baby reacts in this way or if he appears to turn away when you speak or sing to him. Just keep working at your bond – touch your baby gently, speak to him softly, try to keep noise levels down around him and keep the lighting fairly low. In time, he will adjust to his surroundings as he becomes accustomed to this strange new world he has been thrust into.

Baby massage Gentle massage helps your baby to relax while deepening the bonding process.

Dad's turn Giving expressed breast milk from a bottle means dads needn't be excluded from the feeding routine.

Breast still best Breastfeeding is widely accepted as the best form of nutrition for your baby.

the best food The promotion and popularity of baby formula in and around the 1960s made breastfeeding seem passé in many parts of the world for several decades. Now, thanks to a better understanding of the benefits of breast milk and campaigning from groups such as La Lèche League, breastfeeding is once again acknowledged as being the best source of nutrition for babies and is more widely practised than ever. The United Nation's World Health Organization recommends that mothers should be "informed about the superiority and advantages of breastfeeding".

I would urge any mother who is able to breastfeed to do so. Breast milk has many benefits: it is easily digestible, provides ideal nutrition and contains antibodies that help to protect the newborn from infection and disease. Equally importantly, the process of breastfeeding strengthens the bond between mother and child. Dads can also bond with their babies while feeding expressed milk from a bottle. If you are unable to breastfeed, strengthen your bond by holding your baby close, gazing into her eyes and talking soothingly to her while she bottle-feeds.

next to his skin A baby's skin is incredibly sensitive. Nappies and clothing should be made of only the finest natural cotton or other fine natural fibres to avoid skin irritation. Choose clothing that is well-made and avoid fussy garments made from synthetic fabrics. Always keep your baby's comfort the top priority rather than buying clothes you think will make him look cute.

Another issue relating to skin irritation is the way some babies tend to scratch their faces during their first few months as they learn to explore their bodies with their hands. Keep your baby's fingernails short to allow him to explore, rather than covering them. Later on your baby will like to explore his feet, so keep his toenails short, too.

Many infants enjoy the feeling of being snugly bundled up at times. However, as your baby gets older and begins to turn over, crawl, pull himself up and eventually walk, it is best to leave his feet and hands uncovered when he is inside the house to give him the freedom to move around and explore.

Baby clothing Your baby's clothing should be made from natural fibres to prevent skin irritation.

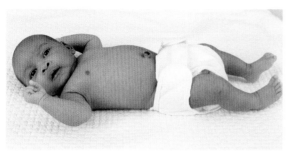

Ditch the disposables Soft cotton nappies are gentler on your baby's skin.

choosing nappies Parents are strongly encouraged to use soft cotton nappies from birth, rather than the disposable ones that have become so common. Three good reasons for this outweigh the extra work of washing nappies or the expense of using a nappy laundry service: first, the widespread use of disposable nappies has built up mountains of slowly decaying material and untreated waste in every city's sanitary landfill; secondly, natural cotton is less irritating to a baby's skin; and finally, babies in cotton nappies can easily sense that they are wet and so learn to recognize when they urinate. This recognition is important when your child is developmentally ready to begin using the toilet (see pages 90–1).

the need to sleep Infants sleep a great deal. Like adults, they sleep to give their bodies rest and to allow their minds to process and integrate the sensory impressions and experiences of the day. Sleep is essential to infants for both their physical well-being and their mental health. Babies will often drift off to sleep when they are tired or if they are overwhelmed with sensory impressions. Until recently, your baby lived inside your womb: a warm, comfortable, dimly lit world with only soft sounds and no rough edges. Now her world is filled with bright lights, loud noises, unexpected movement and strange things that touch her skin. Inevitably, there are times when all of this becomes too much and she switches off and goes to sleep.

Your baby does not need to be held as she goes to sleep. She may, however, like to know that you are close by. You might like to place a large piece of fleece, a small futon or a small mattress for your baby in each room where your family regularly congregates. This allows your baby to be where the action is. She will be comforted to be near you, to hear your voices and to see movement around her. She can look and listen, and then drift off to sleep whenever she is tired.

"Don't wake a sleeping baby" is an old saying, passed down from mother to daughter for generations, and it makes sense! Let your baby sleep. Avoid moving her roughly when she's sleeping, keep the lights down low and speak in soft voices around her.

In on the action Lying on a fleece your baby can feel part of family activities, yet nod off when she needs to sleep.

your
growing baby

In his first year your baby grows and changes rapidly. Take the time to respond to and celebrate each new development.

A new discovery Hands quickly become a major source of interest and exploration for young babies.

Montessori had a simple approach to babies. She believed we should:
• respect all babies as individual human beings
• allow them as much freedom of movement as possible
• help them to become increasingly independent by creating a safe, child-friendly environment that makes it easier for them to explore.

For the first month or so, babies tend to have limited control of their movement. Their arms and legs move jerkily, and they cannot hold their heads upright, which is why we must always be careful to support them. Then, all of a sudden it seems, they discover their hands, feet and faces and are fascinated by them.

By three months, babies can often raise their heads and chests when they are on their stomachs. They make a grab for objects that are dangling and they grasp and shake hand toys. By seven months they are playing with their toes and reaching for objects. Now everything is going into their mouths or is being banged against the floor. With a little help, they can sit up. Babies are usually crawling about on their hands and knees and can pull themselves up to stand by their first birthday. They may be able to take a few steps while they hold onto the furniture, stand alone momentarily and can walk if you hold their hands and walk with them.

In their second year, babies become increasingly mobile and capable. You will start to notice the signs as your child's in-built drive for independence becomes increasingly apparent. For example, he will begin to hold a cup by himself and drink without always making a mess. He will also start to hold out a hand or foot while he is being dressed. It quickly becomes clear, even before your baby begins to move around the house on his own, that redesigning your home environment with your child in mind is going to be very important.

Ready for action Before long, your baby is rolling over and making his first moves towards becoming mobile.

making your home
child-friendly

Even in the early days, babies and small children should
enjoy a strong sense of belonging in the family home.

Made to measure Child-sized
furniture will help your child feel
comfortable in an adult-sized world.

When thinking about how to make our homes more in keeping with the Montessori approach, we need to recognize the significance of the things that we bring into them, especially those our children will experience in their first three years. Young minds absorb all impressions like sponges, and in this period before language develops, their sensory experiences are the sum total of their world. Keep two objectives in mind:

• organize your home to help your child become more independent and self-confident, always keeping health and safety in mind

• design a home that conveys a sense of beauty and order.

Take a look at the size of things in your home. Quite logically, the furniture we use and the way our homes are arranged are designed for adults – sinks and toilets, tables, chairs, sofas and beds are all at a height intended for adults. But babies and young children are very small. Without turning your home topsy-turvy, try to modify the rooms where your family gathers to accommodate your youngest child.

safety matters Safety is, and must always be, a primary concern, but children also need to be given the freedom to move around and explore. Your goal is to prepare your home environment to make it safe for babies

Free to roam Babies need to move about and explore in order to learn. Creating a child-safe environment will mean your baby is free to do this.

and toddlers to do just that, under your supervision, but without you having to worry every minute that something terrible is about to happen. Many parents are overly concerned about safety and this leads them to confine their young children in restrictive baby and toddler devices, such as cribs, playpens, baby seats, highchairs, swings, pushchairs and the like. It is not uncommon to see a child strapped into a baby carrier, which snaps into a car seat, which in turn snaps into a pushchair, allowing the child to be carried around without any physical movement or contact.

On one level it sounds reasonable to confine children because of safety concerns, but parents also need to understand that every hour spent confined in a baby carrier is an opportunity lost. Given more freedom, their babies could have been developing muscular coordination and strength, along with the sensory stimulation of hands-on learning. By paying meticulous attention to making your home child-safe, you can create an environment in which your child is free to move about and explore without you having to worry.

safety sense

There are many different products on the market that help make your home safer. Here are just a few things to remember:

- **Cover all electrical sockets** within reach of your growing child.
- **Install safety gates** to secure your child's bedroom, stairways and any rooms that you do not want her to enter (or leave).
- **Secure or remove any wires** that run across the floor or anywhere else where your growing child might reach them.
- **Some houseplants are poisonous** if eaten. Remove them.
- **Remove or lock cabinets or cupboards** where you store chemicals, tools, forks, knives and other potentially dangerous items.
- **Use the safety lock** or switch on your oven if it has one! Keep saucepan handles to the back of the hob when cooking.
- **Bathrooms can be dangerous** (especially toilets, hairdryers, razors and the like). Secure your bathroom from unsupervised exploration, and keep cabinets containing medicines locked at all times.

planning the perfect
first bedroom

Create an organized yet interesting first bedroom that will be fun
as well as safe for your baby to explore once he is on the move.

Bedroom basics Your baby's
first bedroom should be bright
and colourful, clean and orderly.

Babies absorb everything that surrounds them in their environment. They
are acutely aware of colours, patterns, sounds, textures and aromas. When
planning your baby's first bedroom you will want to provide an environment
that is filled with beauty. It should be bright and colourful, clean and
orderly. With this in mind, look at the room from your baby's perspective.
Get down on the floor. What do you see? What can you hear? The first
few weeks and months will be the time in your baby's life when everything
is fresh and new, and lifelong impressions will be made. Bring together
elements that are well-made and chosen for their beauty.

visual stimulation At birth, babies' eyes tend to focus on
objects that are fairly close, but they can also see and are stimulated by
something that is further away, especially if it moves. One of the first
things babies see and focus on instinctively is the human face. Your
presence and interaction with your baby is a powerful source of visual
stimulation. As the days go by, his interest in the sights around him grows.
Hang a mobile over your baby's bed and nappy-changing area so he has
something to observe. Homemade mobiles that can be added to allow you
to change what your child is looking at from time to time.

artwork Decorate the walls of your child's room with pictures hung very low on the wall (equivalent to eye-level when he is old enough to toddle). Avoid the typical cartoons and commercial images from television and films. Choose framed art prints or posters that show lovely scenes with children and animals. During these years of acute sensitivity, it's worth exposing your child to good art and beautiful objects.

musical value Today, many parents realize the value of exposing young children to good music. Music should be an important part of every child's life. Set some space aside, out of your baby's reach, for a simple stereo system and collection of recordings and play music for your baby to listen to. Select music that has simple melodies and clearly defined instrumentation when possible, such as recordings of a bamboo flute, a classical guitar or a harp. Don't overstimulate your baby with loud music – play it at a moderate volume.

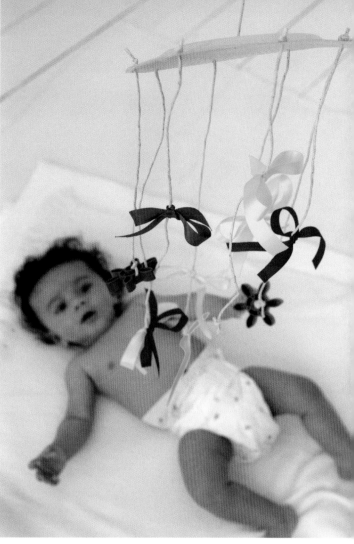

First impressions Stimulate your baby's vision with a mobile hung over his bed or nappy-changing area.

beautiful toys Babies do not need many toys in the early months, other than a few rattles and a stuffed animal or two. But as the months pass by, you will probably find your child begins to accumulate more. There is no need to buy expensive battery-operated toys, especially for children under the age of three. Instead, look for toys which are beautifully made that your child can stack, assemble or interact with in one way or another. Avoid any toy that simply does something while your child watches. You want to encourage your child to be actively engaged, not a passive observer waiting to be entertained.

Choose well-made wooden toys rather than the plastic variety found in every modern toy shop. Remember that your very young child is in a sensitive period during which he is forming strong sensory impressions. Plastic toys are more or less unbreakable and they are relatively inexpensive,

Easy access A low bed or futon placed on the floor will give your baby more freedom once she is mobile.

Space to play Instead of confining your baby to a playpen, put a stairgate across her bedroom doorway creating a larger and more interesting play area.

but they do not appeal to children in the way that beautifully made wooden ones can and they tend to be treated carelessly. One of our goals is to instill a sense of appreciation for beautiful things in our children from the earliest years, while at the same time cultivating a sense of order.

Instead of using a toy box, keep toys neatly on shelves. If a toy consists of lots of small parts keep them together in a basket.

an infant and toddler bed
For your baby's first bed you will need a crib or, alternatively, consider placing a small futon or mattress on the floor. A low bed of this sort will be just the right height for your child to crawl out of and back into when she is old enough to move around. Freely exploring her bedroom, assuming that you have made it completely safe, is much more interesting than being confined to a crib. Your child's entire bedroom can become a safe play area – all you need is a stairgate across the doorway, safety covers for your electrical outlets and some careful thought about what you bring into the bedroom while your child is young. Use sheets and blankets for your baby's bed, progressing to pillows and duvets only when your child is at least one year old.

A low futon with a waterproof covering is also a safe alternative to the traditional nappy-changing table – it isn't difficult to imagine your baby falling off a changing table once she can wriggle around.

Tidy toys Keep your child's toys on shelves she can easily reach rather than putting them away in a toy box.

adapting your home to a
growing child

As your child becomes more independent and busy, try to accommodate her activities wherever the family gathers.

"young children have a tremendous need and love for an orderly environment"

Left to their own devices, young children may tend to create chaos, but they also have a tremendous need and love for an orderly environment. Try to arrange the rooms where your child spends most of her time to make it easy for her to maintain a neat, well-organized atmosphere. It's surprising what an impact this can have on her developing personality.

in the family room

Family room, living room, playroom – whatever you call it, families tend to congregate in one room in the house. Plan yours with your child in mind. It should include accessible shelves where she can keep books and toys neatly and attractively organized. Avoid putting out too many toys and books at one time. Divide toys into three or more sets: favourites, which are kept out on the shelves continually, and two or more sets that are rotated in and out of the toy cupboard every month or so.

Provide a child-sized table and chairs where your child can work on neat projects. Furniture should be at the right height to support good posture while your child reads, writes and works. Include a basket holding some small rugs that can be spread out to define your child's work areas when she chooses to play on the floor (see page 83).

Child-friendly space Accessible shelving and baskets for storage allow children to maintain an organized environment for themselves.

Kitchen craft A child-sized work table in your kitchen allows your child to work and play alongside you.

in the kitchen

If at all possible, once your child reaches about two years of age make room in your kitchen for a child-sized work table for young cooks. Use a bottom drawer to store forks, knives and spoons and a low shelf to hold your child-sized plates, bowls, glasses and napkins. Set aside the bottom shelf in your fridge for your child. Here you can store small drink jugs, pieces of fruit and the ingredients she might need for making snacks. Use non-breakable plastic containers to hold peanut butter, jams, lunchmeats and spreads. A child of two is capable of opening the fridge and taking out her own prepared snack or cold drink stored in a cup. A slightly older child can pour her own juice from a jug and make her own snack (see pages 104–5). Prepared snacks, such as yogurt, can be bought in small individual servings and stored on this shelf.

in the bathroom

Cast your eye around your bathroom to see how you can make it easier for your child to use what she needs to. She should be able to reach the sink, turn on the taps and reach her toothbrush and toothpaste without help. There should be a special place where her towel and facecloth are kept so she can reach them. Most parents provide bathroom stools, but small, wobbly stools do not provide enough secure, comfortable space for bathroom tasks. If possible, build or buy a sturdy wooden platform 15–20cm (6-8in) high that fits around the toilet and sink.

Step up Children need to be able to reach the sink – make sure your bathroom step is sturdy and solid.

in the hall

Make your hall child-friendly by providing a low bench where your children can leave their shoes neatly pegged together and position coat hooks at a level that children can reach by themselves.

in the bedroom

As your child reaches the age of two, you could either continue to allow her to sleep on a futon or buy a bed that is low to the floor. This makes it easy and safe for your child to get into and out of bed on her own, and helps to give her a sense of independence. As long as your child is more than one year old, you may choose to allow her to use a duvet or sleeping bag on her bed instead of sheets and blankets. This makes it much easier for her to make her own bed in the morning.

In addition to providing child-sized furniture, make sure your child can reach door knobs and light switches without help. Light switches can be modified with extenders to allow your child to turn lights on and off independently – these are sold in most hardware shops.

Plan your child's bedroom up to a point, but then let it reflect her personality and current interests. As well as space to play with toys, provide an art table for non-messy art work, such as drawing or paper and paste projects. Hang a bulletin board low on the wall so your child can hang her own artwork. Small shelves and tables also make good display areas.

Music should be an important part of every child's life. Provide a simple stereo system and give your child a step-by-step demonstration on how to use it carefully and sensibly.

Hall order Easy-to-reach coat hooks, a low bench and a stool help your child to get ready by herself.

An orderly environment When everything has its set place your child can easily maintain order in her room.

You and your child may like to create a model town or farm on a piece of heavy plywood. With it placed on a low table, your child can create wonderful displays with model buildings made of wood or plastic.

Avoid clutter. Place toys with many pieces in appropriate containers, such as plastic boxes with lids or small baskets. Have a look at the shelves in our Montessori classroom (see pages 18–21) and try to duplicate the look. Store building blocks in a colourful and sturdy canvas bag with handles. Sew on strips of Velcro to fasten the bag closed. When you travel it is easy to pick the bag up and take it with you.

bedroom design

Open storage Small baskets are ideal for toys with lots of pieces and enable your child to tidy up herself.

Crayon box Keep crayons sharpened and stored in a box that is easy for your child to reach and carry around.

Nature's display Provide space for a nature museum where your child can collect natural objects he has found.

Basketware Instead of a chest of drawers, install a low shelf unit on which you can place small baskets for socks and underwear.

Low shelving Store toys on low shelves, then set up a rotation system so that not all her toys are available for playing with at the same time.

Coat rack Mount a coat rack low on one wall so your child can hang up his coat, hat and dressing gown, and get them down easily by himself.

an arts and crafts area

Most of us are anxious to encourage our children's creativity. Every home with young children benefits from some sort of arts and crafts area. This might be in a corner of the kitchen, your child's bedroom, or a hallway – really it can be any place where you are comfortable allowing your child to work with art materials, such as paints and pastels, which obviously can spill and stain. You will probably want to choose an area with a tile floor so that spills can be easily cleaned up, or you can lay down a large plastic drop cloth.

It is a good idea to set up an easel for painting and an art table covered with a washable tablecloth for drawing, craftwork and working with clay.

Paint Fred puts on his plastic overall, spreads out newspaper and pours his paint into wide-necked pots.

Paper It took some practise at first, but Fred is now able to attach a sheet of paper to his easel with a clip.

Pots Fred lets the drips fall from his brush and scrapes the excess paint on the edge of the pot before he starts.

A small shelf unit at a height your child can reach can be used to store his art supplies, brushes, paper and so on. You might want to add in a freestanding clothes-drying rack so your child can hang up his finished paintings to dry with clothes pegs. Once the arts and crafts area is set up, show your child how to proceed using the same step-by-step process each time for getting started and for clearing up when he has finished.

Children's art supplies can be neatly stored in separate plastic containers. Depending on your child's age, the art supplies that you prepare might

Getting started "This is the house we all stayed in on holiday," Fred tells his mum as he paints. When he has finished he uses clothes pegs to hang his picture on a drying rack, puts lids on the pots and washes out his brushes.

include washable magic markers, crayons, paste, paper, fabric scraps and recycled household articles for making collages. You can keep tempera paint fresh once it is mixed by storing it in plastic containers which can be sealed with lids. It is important to provide the very best art materials – paints, brushes, drawing pencils, crayons, paper and such like – that you can afford, and to teach your child how to use them correctly and how to take care of them, including how to store them properly when they are not being used.

KEY
IDEA

watch and follow
your child

As parents we often feel the need to direct our children,
but Montessori believed we should follow them instead.

Making notes Keep a journal of
your child's activities and achievements.

How much time do you spend watching your child? I don't mean watching half-heartedly while you are doing something else. I mean focusing your attention completely on your child for an extended period of time. There is no better way to begin using Montessori's principles in your home than by sitting back and observing what your child is looking at, what he says and what he does. Children have so much to teach us about their needs and interests if we will only take the time to pay attention.

how to observe
You may find it useful to keep a bound notebook or journal in which you can make notes and keep a record of your observations. Regularly set aside some time to observe your child. Sit somewhere comfortable close to him so that you can easily see and hear him and any other children with whom he is playing. Make notes every so often about what you see – these will accumulate to form an interesting record of your child's behaviour at different ages, as well as helping you to notice if a pattern of behaviour is emerging at a particular time. Try to interpret what your child's behaviour means. When you notice a new fascination, think about ways to introduce some new activities that will feed and extend this interest.

what to observe

Remember, the only thing that you can count on day after day with children is that as they grow their preferences, interests and abilities change in unpredictable ways. Every time you observe your child, try to forget about previous experiences or perceptions and focus on what is really happening right now.

While your child is playing, notice which toys he selects. How does he use them? Does he tend to play alone or with others? Do you notice any patterns over time? Observe how your child moves about the house. Does he move from place to place quietly and gracefully or with considerable disruption? Is there a room in your home that your child prefers to be in? What seems to attract him to that room?

When eating, note what your child most enjoys. Can he drink without spilling and use a fork, knife and spoon appropriately and with good hand-eye coordination? How does your child behave at mealtimes? Is this a time when he likes to talk about his day?

As you observe, think twice before you interfere with anything your child is doing. Your goal in this exercise is to learn from what he is doing, not to keep jumping up and correcting him.

On a mission Watch how your child moves about the house – is she quiet and graceful or noisy and disruptive?

CHAPTER
TWO

discovery
through
the senses

KEY
IDEA

building sensory
awareness

There is an old saying that children learn what they live.
Essentially, Montessori is saying the same thing.

"encourage
young children
to focus their
attention more
carefully on the
physical world"

We have already seen how babies interact with the world around them through their senses from the moment of birth. Montessori believed that we can build on this and encourage babies and young children to focus their attention more carefully on the physical world, exploring with each of their senses – sight, hearing, taste, touch and smell – subtle variations in the properties of given collections of objects. Exercising children's senses, by drawing their attention to aspects of everyday life or through specific sensorial activities, can greatly improve their awareness.

boosting brain power
In the years from birth to six, exercises to develop sensory awareness are especially valuable because this is when the nervous system is developing. As we stimulate children's senses in ways that require them to notice and discriminate between the properties of different objects, signals are sent from the nervous system to the brain and back again. The more this happens, the stronger the neuropathways in the brain become, as the brain receives important stimulation that is essential to proper functioning. Learning how to learn (the assimilation, integration and application of knowledge) later in life depends on whether or not the brain was properly "hard-wired" from an early age.

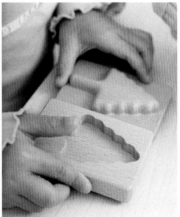

Journey of discovery Learning how to do simple puzzles challenges your child's spatial awareness.

Simple smells Encourage your child to enjoy the sensory delights of the world around her.

how babies experience
their world

As the early months pass by, babies increasingly look at, listen to, pick up, taste and smell almost anything that comes into their environment.

"your child's sensory education began at birth as you held her in your arms"

Your child's sensory education began at birth as you held her in your arms for the first time, and cuddled her against you. Her exposure to sensory experiences continued as she took in the comforting aroma of your skin; the sights and sounds and smells of everything around her; the touch of clothing against her tender skin; and the taste of the first solid foods that passed through her lips.

Babies are keen observers in their first few years of life. Everything a baby sees will make an impression, stimulating the brain and nervous system, as well as impacting on the baby's sense of safety and security.

keen vision One way we prepare our home environment for babies is by selecting things that will visually stimulate them. It helps, though, to understand something about how vision develops in babies.

When they are born, and for the first month or so, babies' eyes tend to focus on objects about a foot away. If you watch closely, you'll probably notice that your baby's eyes wander and may even cross from time to time. Of all the things they may see, they respond to the sight of the human face most of all, especially the faces of their parents and any other primary care givers. They tend not to notice subtle colours or shading and seem to pay

Sensorial start Touching, hearing and smelling mum signal the start of a child's sensory education.

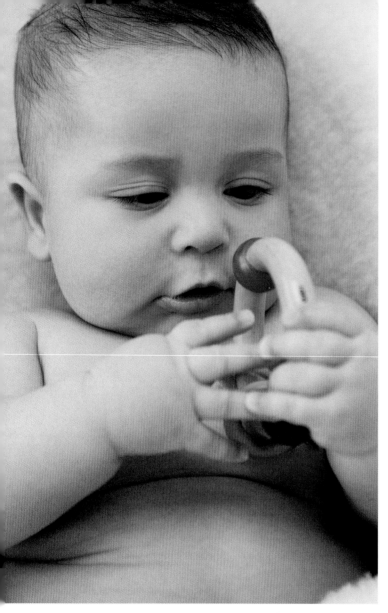

Look and learn Young babies are keen to explore with their eyes and hands in the early months of life.

the most attention to things that show clear patterns with high contrast, especially things that are black and white.

At about three months old, babies are beginning to focus on things that are further away. They will watch people's faces intently. Their eyes follow moving objects. Now they can recognize familiar people and objects at a distance. They begin to reach for things that they see. By about seven months they have developed full colour vision and fairly mature distance vision. They can easily track moving objects with their eyes.

There are all sorts of things that you can do to help develop your child's visual perceptiveness. Talk to your baby, and when you do, make direct eye contact with her and notice how she responds. Look at things together and talk about what you see. Mobiles, as they slowly spin, present an everchanging view of interesting objects that are moving. You might like to have two or three around the house and rotate them every so often to create interest and delight in the new sights.

musical impact Listening to music is an important sensorial experience. You can introduce your baby to music in many ways. Some parents begin by playing recorded music to their developing baby during pregnancy, sensing that their unborn child can hear sounds and rhythms, just as we can when we are underwater.

"your baby will use her hands, eyes, ears, mouth and nose to investigate everything that crosses her path"

In the early years, the experience of hearing recorded music is certainly taken in by babies and young children and is stored as part of the ongoing stimulation of the environment. Talk and sing to your baby from birth. Melodies and lullabies are important and become deep-rooted memories of early childhood. The sound and rhythm of the music that you play in your young child's room and the words to familiar songs that she will begin to learn as she gets older, all lay the foundations for a music education.

Music has also been shown to be directly connected to the development of those areas in the brain that are associated with mathematics and pattern recognition. In other words, music not only makes children more artistically sensitive, it makes a very real contribution to their brain's development.

hand to mouth From her very first feed, your baby's mouth becomes a source of exploration and pleasure. Weaning your baby is about much more than introducing solid food – each new food generates interest and excitement as your baby explores tastes and textures. As she grows, every object within her reach will go straight into her mouth.

getting a balance In no time at all your baby is able to pick up objects and explore their weight, texture and temperature. She will use her hands, eyes, ears, mouth and nose to investigate everything that crosses her path. And by the time she is one year old your child will become increasingly curious and able to focus and concentrate, watching or examining something that catches her attention with infinite patience.

It is important to avoid over or under stimulation – babies are good at letting us know how they are feeling. Too much stimulation and they become stressed and go to sleep. They also fall asleep when there is too little stimulation. Ideally, we need to establish a good balance.

Tastes good By six months, everything within reach seems to end up in your baby's mouth.

basket of
treasures

All around your baby is a magical world
of objects just waiting to be discovered.

Once your baby is able to sit and hold things she will love to explore a
"treasure basket". This is a low basket or sturdy box you have filled with
lots of interesting household objects and things from nature. The objects
must be large enough not to be swallowed and free from sharp edges or
anything else that might be harmful when they are touched and quite
possibly mouthed by a young child. Older toddlers enjoy the treasure
basket, too – just keep introducing new objects.

what's inside? A treasure basket should create a sense of wonder,
surprise and discovery. Gather between 50 and 100 objects, each of which
has distinctly different characteristics: shape, colour, texture, weight and
smell – use your imagination and common sense. You might include
things such as a wallet, a large walnut shell, a pine cone, a brush, a feather,
a silver bell, a smooth stone. Babies and toddlers use all of their senses,
whereas adults tend to rely on sight. Objects that have a distinct visual
pattern or texture on their surface, a distinct aroma, that are cool to the
touch (such as a stone) or which make a noise when moved are especially
intriguing. To a young child, everything is a new and exciting discovery.

Treasure trove The treasures in this basket fascinate young children. They will return to explore them over and over again.

ideas for treasure

- **metal:** plug and chain • bell
- measuring spoon • small whisk
- **natural:** pine cone • sponge
- avocado stone • feather • large
pebble • shell
- **wooden:** spoon • wooden egg
- pastry brush • clothes peg • brick
- shoe brush
- **glass:** egg cup • spice jar • salt
cellar • small paperweight • string
of beads
- **fabric and leather:** satin and
velvet ribbons • ball of wool
- small purse • silk scarf • pompom
- keyholder

objects to avoid

- small choking hazards • objects
with sharp edges • objects with
loose threads or pieces • anything
that might be harmful if mouthed
- materials with non-colourfast dyes

Objective investigation One enticing object often has particular appeal and becomes the most precious. Your baby will return to it time and time again to examine its properties and see what she can make of it.

The treasure basket can entertain young children for long periods of time: half an hour would not be unusual. With babies, keep in mind that it is very stimulating, so is best offered when your child is rested and alert. When young children are first exploring the basket it is best not to say a word – just select an object, carefully examine it and put it back in the basket. Your child may reach for it as soon as you put it down or she may choose something altogether different. Allow her to explore things on her own. Children like us to be nearby, but they do not always want us to interfere.

TASTING Sucking has been a source of great satisfaction for your baby since birth so expect every object in the basket to be sampled in her mouth. As long as objects are clean and safe, you don't need to limit this experience – your baby will decide what tastes good and what doesn't.

LOOKING Sharp contrasts were important in the early days when her vision was still developing but your baby now has adult acuity. She can appreciate natural colours, subtle shades and combinations of shapes. A simple household item such as a pastry brush can have great appeal.

HEARING Beans and seeds in small sealed bottles and jars make interesting sounds, as do tiny bells or crackly paper inside tightly tied drawstring bags. Metal chains, strings of beads and measuring spoons clatter against other objects and jangle when they are shaken.

TOUCHING Things that have a distinct visual pattern or texture on their surface, such as a pine cone, are especially intriguing. Glass objects and polished pebbles are interestingly cool to touch, unlike plastic toys, which all feel the same.

EXPLORING When your child has exhausted the possibilities of the treasure, there is still a textured basket to be investigated. Your baby may spend 20 or 30 minutes exploring the contents of the basket – allow her to decide when she has had enough.

SMELLING Your baby has a highly developed sense of smell and will appreciate some carefully chosen scents in the basket. Try bags of herbs, sachets of lavender and a lemon. Or put scented sweets, vanilla pods or coffee beans inside a salt cellar.

sensory activities that help
children learn

Exercises that develop children's sensory awareness help them to appreciate their world much more fully for the rest of their lives.

"the sensory exercises are just difficult enough to represent a meaningful challenge"

It is important to continue to educate young senses. I don't believe that we can physically improve them through sensory awareness training, but I do think we can help children learn to see, hear, touch, taste or smell what they experience with a deeper appreciation. In the Montessori classroom an entire area of the curriculum is devoted to sensory awareness training.

At the most simple level, the exercises challenge children to find identical pairs of objects that vary by only one aspect, such as height, length or width. Other exercises ask them to find identical pairs based on weight, aroma, taste, temperature or sound. At a more advanced level, children are asked to arrange a set of objects in order based on the variation in one aspect, such as length, height, colour tone, shape and so on.

Children find these puzzles and games interesting because they are just difficult enough to represent a meaningful challenge. They are also vocabulary lessons, as the children master the names of everything from geometric shapes to plants and animals. As children learn the correct names for things, the objects themselves take on new meaning.

The activities in this chapter are simpler than those found in Montessori schools, but are based on the same principles. Many of the items used can be made at home or bought from specialist stockists (see page 188).

Guitar girl As she plucks and strums the strings of the guitar, Imogen experiments with the different sounds they make.

Colour coded Sorting buttons by colour stimulates sight and touch.

Button mix You can vary the challenge by introducing buttons of different sizes and shapes, or made of different materials, such as bone, wood and metal.

colour, shape and size

Many play activities that primarily stimulate your child's sight will require him to use other senses simultaneously.

sorting objects (2–5 years)

Sorting objects according to shape, size, colour or other physical properties is a wonderful activity that challenges young children to pay close attention and to make some logical choices. For this activity, you will want to gather several examples of some sort of appealing object in various shapes, colours and sizes. Be careful with small objects as your toddler can swallow them or they can end up in his nostrils or ears.

A good example of this activity is button sorting. Buy some buttons from a hardware shop or select several different sets of four or more identical buttons from your sewing box, if you have one. Mix the buttons together in a large bowl then show your child how to select one button, place it in a smaller bowl and then find each of the other buttons that is the same.

step by step: pink block tower

ONE Working on a small rug, Lauren looks for the largest stacking cube.

TWO It takes a few attempts before she gets the biggest cube at the bottom.

THREE Once this cube is in place, Lauren looks for the next biggest.

FOUR Before long, Lauren sees her tower quickly growing.

FIVE Taking great care, she positions the smaller pieces near the top.

SIX And finally, with the smallest piece in place, Lauren's tower is built.

stacking cubes (18 months–3 years)

A good visual sensorial activity to use with young children involves a set of wooden stacking cubes that are graduated in size. In Montessori schools, we use a set called the Pink Tower. For your home you can buy graduated blocks or cups that nest inside each other and build into a tower in the same way.

Wooden puzzle Choose puzzles with simple cut-out shapes and with an individual knob for each piece.

geometric shape stacker (2–4 years)

There are many variations of this toy but most have one or more spindles and sets of pieces. Once the pieces are removed, the challenge is for your child to find the pieces that are alike: squares, octagons and circles, for example. Then she finds the largest piece within that set, and places it on the spindle at the bottom. She continues until all of the pieces have been placed. Your child should be able to recognize for herself if she has made a mistake because a larger piece placed over a smaller one will hang over, and it will not look right.

simple puzzles (2–5 years)

Simple puzzles are a time-honoured toy for young children. Always look for puzzles made from wood with attractive images. Avoid puzzles made of cardboard and those that do not fit into a frame for each piece. When your child is under the age of four, look for puzzles that have a large knob for each piece.

matching coloured paint charts (3–5 years)

Montessori schools use prepared sets of wooden tablets painted with various colours to help children learn to distinguish between primary and secondary colours and tones, while also mastering the words used to describe each colour and shade. You can do this at home by gathering paint charts from your local DIY store.

You can create three separate sets of colours from the charts. Each set should be the same size, differing only in colour. For younger children start with a set of six colours, two each of yellow, red and blue. Ask your child to match the pairs and learn the spoken names of these primary colours.

When your child can manage these, collect a second set of 11 pairs of the primary and secondary colours and tones: yellow, red, blue, green, orange, purple, pink, brown, grey, white and black. Invite your child to match and name them. For a more difficult challenge, build a third set containing seven different shades of each of nine different colours (yellow, red, blue, green, orange, purple, pink, brown, grey), which your child learns to sort in order from the lightest to the darkest shade. When all of the charts are laid out in an array it creates a lovely display of colour.

There are many ways in which you can make this work more challenging. For example, ask your child to find the colour on the chart that is closest in colour to something in the room. Another challenge is to show your child a colour from the third set of colours and ask him, by memory alone, to point out the colour on the chart that is just one shade lighter or darker. A third activity, with older children, would be to teach them how to create lighter or darker shades of paint by adding white or black paint to an existing colour. By beginning with the pure colour and adding a bit more white and mixing it up, they can create a series of daubs of paint from darkest to lightest, similar to the paint charts.

concentration game (3–5 years)

This game helps children develop their visual memory and pattern recognition skills. You can buy various versions at most toy shops or you can make your own. To make a set, cut out 16 pieces of thin cardboard the size of standard playing cards. Either draw or cut out two identical copies of eight different geometric shapes. Pictures of animals can also be used. Glue a shape or picture on to each card. You should now have 16 identical-sized cards, made up of eight pairs of different shapes or pictures.

Matching pairs Remembering where pairs of identical cards are tests memory and concentration.

To play the game, mix up the cards and place them face down in a square made up of four rows down with four cards across in each row. The first player turns over two cards, one at a time. If they match, that player keeps the pair. If they do not match, the player turns them face down again. Players attempt to remember which card is in each position, making it more likely that they will find matching cards when it is their next turn. The game continues until all cards have been matched.

As your child gets better at this game, you can make new sets with different designs or images, and you can increase the challenge by adding more pairs to the set and by not arranging them in rows.

Bean cascade Butter beans make a pleasant sound when dropped from a ladle into a bowl.

sound

As your child gets older and his hearing develops, he can learn to distinguish between different sounds and also to pinpoint where a sound is coming from.

dried butter beans (18 months–4 years)

Find a large salad bowl that is made of heavy pottery or glass and half fill it with dried beans. Dried butter beans are good as they are too large to go into your child's nose or ears, and they make a pleasant sound when dropped into the bowl. Give your child a small ladle and show him how to use it to scoop up some beans, then empty the ladle back into the bowl. Allow very young children to play with the beans. As they swish their hands around, the beans make an interesting sound. If your child knocks some out, show him how to pick them up and return them to the bowl. Stress the importance of getting all the beans back into the bowl. At first, don't be surprised if the beans spill all around. Show your child the correct way to put them back using patient, kind language.

matching bells (2–5 years)

For this activity you will need to gather eight or more pairs of bells, each pair having the same sound. Because the bells may look different, your child will need to do this activity with her eyes closed or blindfolded. You are likely to find two types of bells: those with handles and those that are normally sewn or fixed onto something, such as clothing or a horse's harness. The second type is difficult for small children to work with because the ring is muffled by their hands as they hold it. You can solve this by tying a ribbon to the bell. Your child picks it up by the ribbon with one hand and shakes it or strikes it with the other hand to get it to ring.

Ringing bells Recognizing the sounds made by matching pairs of bells is a good auditory activity.

Your child rings one bell and sets it aside. She then picks up another bell and rings it to see if it is the same. She may want to ring the first bell again to refresh her memory. If the first bell she tried is not the right match, she sets it aside, selects another and listens to that one for a match. When she finds the right bell, she can set the two matching bells to one side together. She then goes on to select another bell, and repeats the process until she finds the match for each bell.

Matching sounds See if your child can match the sounds made by various objects in pairs of containers.

sound cylinders (3–6 years)

Another exercise which helps children develop the ability to discriminate between sounds involves using a set of sound cylinders. You can make these from any wooden, plastic or glass containers that you find around the house. The containers need to be opaque so you cannot see what's inside, and they need to produce a clear sound when they are filled with different objects and shaken. Small glass jars, such as the ones that baby food comes in, can be used if you paint the insides or line them with coloured paper to make the walls opaque.

Six containers should be painted one colour, and the other six a second colour. Fill pairs of the jars (one jar of each colour) with something that will make an interesting sound when rattled or shaken (dried peas, beans, rice, sand). The children then try to match each green cylinder with the pink cylinder of the same sound. In Montessori schools, each set of six jars of one colour is housed in a box with a lid painted in the same colour.

the silence game (2–6 years)

In our modern world, it seems that silence is almost unknown. It is a great gift to help your children discover the beauty that can be found in silence. When silent we can hear our own thoughts, and we also become much more aware of the world around us.

The silence game helps children develop a much higher level of self-discipline, along with a greater awareness of the sounds around them that most people take for granted. In this activity, get your children's attention either by ringing a small bell or by giving a familiar hand signal to begin a game of "silence". Your children should stop what they are doing, sit down, close their eyes and try to remain perfectly still. Challenge them to stay like this until they hear you whisper their name. When each child hears his or her name spoken softly, he or she should silently rise and join you. You might want to vary the silence game and help your children learn to move carefully and quickly by challenging them to carry bells across the room without allowing them to ring.

At first, younger children may not be able to remain still and silent for more than 30 seconds, but gradually they will develop the ability to relax, listen and appreciate the silence. If your children enjoy this game, make it a daily ritual. Another variation is guided visualization: a process by which your children close their eyes and you describe a scene in front of them for them to imagine. "Now we are walking down to the brook. We put in our toe. Oh my, the water is so cold!"

"gradually children develop the ability to relax, listen and appreciate silence"

listening to music (18 months–6 years)

As your child gets older, you can play all sorts of musical games with her. You can sing or hum loudly along with the music, encouraging your child to do so, too. You can clap your hands to the beat and you can dance free style in response to music, swaying, twirling gently or dancing in any way that feels right for the music playing.

Start to teach your child to recognize the instruments that are being played in a particular piece of music, as well as teaching her the name of the tune – "Mummy, *Swan Lake* is playing on the radio!" – or even the composer. Make sure your child has access to lots of instruments that she can play – maracas, xylophone, drums, guitar – and encourage her to sing along with favourite tunes.

Remember that, during these years, your child is in a sensitive period for music and has a spontaneous interest in the development of pitch, rhythm and melody. Musically talented parents who expose their children to live music in their home life tend to find they produce children who are musically gifted, and Suzuki music teachers have shown for years that children younger than the age of four can learn to play an instrument, such as the piano or violin.

Music matters Encourage your child to listen to all types of music and to clap, dance and sing along.

touch

There are many ways to train children's sense of touch. We began with the basket of treasures (see pages 56–9) when our children were very young. Now they are ready to attempt some more challenging activities as they start to refine this sense.

texture matching (2–5 years)

This game is ideal for helping to develop your child's sense of touch. Typically, it consists of a set of small tablets or squares of wood with a distinct texture on one face, created by gluing a piece of fabric, Velcro, seeds, sand or other substance to that surface. You will need two matching squares for each texture, creating pairs that feel the same when touched. When the textured side is turned downwards, the squares all look the same. With his eyes closed or blindfolded, ask your child to try to "see" with his fingertips, finding the matching pairs. When turned over, the textured sides of each pair match, providing a visual key so your child can see if he has guessed correctly.

Mix and match Fill a basket with pairs of different fabrics and see if your child can find the matching pairs with his eyes closed, using his sense of touch.

fabric matching (2–5 years)

A variation on the concept above involves a basket filled with squares of different kinds of fabrics: silk, wool, cotton, tweed and such like. Prepare matching pairs of each type of fabric. With his eyes closed or blindfolded, ask your child to try to find the pairs of fabric squares that feel the same and to lay them together on the table. When he opens his eyes, he can check his work by looking at the squares.

sandpaper tablets (3–5 years)

The sandpaper tablets consist of a set of six pairs of wooden tablets with each pair covered with a different grade of sandpaper. Your child attempts to identify pairs that have the same roughness, working by touch alone with his eyes closed or blindfolded. When he has finished matching the tablets, he can check his work by turning them over. The matching pairs will look the same.

step by step: the mystery bag

Mystery objects Choose objects to go inside the mystery bag that have distinctive sizes, shapes and textures that you know your child will recognize.

ONE Georgia puts her hand into the bag and feels the mystery object.

TWO She calls out what she thinks it is before pulling it out of the bag.

the mystery bag (3–6 years)

The mystery bag has long been a favourite children's activity. Usually it is simply a cloth bag or box with a hole for your child's hands, through which she can touch and manipulate objects that she cannot see. To play, you will need a collection of small objects with which your child is familiar and which she can name. While she closes her eyes, place an object inside the bag and challenge her to identify it by touch alone. If your child guesses correctly, you and your child change roles. Keep this game going for older children by making it more difficult using different coins, shells or geometric shapes, for example.

Scent bottles Comparing and matching scents in bottles helps develop your child's sense of smell.

smell

Children have a much more sensitive sense of smell than most adults. Here are two exercises to help your child refine her perceptions and learn to recognize and name different aromas.

scent bottles (3–5 years)

These consist of a set of 12 small, identical plastic or glass containers with lids. Cylindrical spice jars with screw-on caps are ideal, but you can also use baby food jars. You are going to create two identical sets of six jars. Cover one set of jars with blue paper and the other set with green paper.

Put a cotton wool ball inside each jar and place a drop or two of the same scent on the ball of one green and one blue jar. Use different scents for each of the six pairs of jars. You might use aromatic liquid flavourings such as vanilla, almond, peppermint, lemon, eau de cologne or a perfume. In some, you could skip the cotton wool ball and use something solid that has a strong and pleasant scent, such as potpourri, spices such as cloves or cinnamon, or orange or lemon rinds. In this case, you need to be sure that your child cannot see what is in the jar. Remember, these substances will dry out and lose their aroma after a while, so you will need to refresh them from time to time.

Your child selects a jar from one set, opens the lid and sniffs the scent. She then finds the matching jar from the other set. She sets the two jars aside and repeats the process with the remaining jars.

herb scents (3–5 years)

If you have a herb garden, your child will enjoy smelling aromatic herbs such as rosemary, lavender, basil and thyme. It will be even more satisfying if she has grown these herself (see page 139). Show her how to use a small mortar and pestle to crush the herbs, or even how to make sachets or bowls with potpourri that add a pleasant fragrance to your home.

"children have a much more sensitive sense of smell than most adults"

Fruit flavours Eating fresh fruit salad is a multi-sensory experience for your child, full of colour, scents, tastes and even sounds made as he takes each bite.

taste

There are four basic tastes that we can sense with our tongue: sweet, sour, salty and bitter. The most basic way to introduce the concept of taste is to talk about different foods: "Mmmm, this apple is so sweet!" or "I think this popcorn is very salty! What do you think?" Some children are quite fussy about eating foods that have a strong or unfamiliar flavour. You may find that your child becomes more willing to try new foods as he explores new scents and tastes through sensory experiences. To start with, gradually introduce each taste with different foods. For example, you might introduce bitter by offering your child a tiny bit of horseradish or some parsley. "Some foods taste bitter. Would you like to try my ....?"

Another activity would be to suggest that your child pays close attention to the taste of certain foods. "Goodness, just taste and smell the ginger in this gingerbread cookie!" You can suggest that your child closes his eyes, takes a taste of something and tries to name what the taste is. "This is very lemony, Mummy!" You can also make tasting bottles (see panel right).

tasting bottles
(3–5 years)

Gather eight small bottles with squeeze droppers and paint the lids of four bottles blue and the other four red. Now you have two sets of four dropper bottles. Fill one bottle from each set with a liquid that represents one of the four basic tastes. For example, sugar water (sweet), lemon juice (sour), salty water (salty) and black coffee diluted with water (bitter).

Your child should wash her hands, line up each set of bottles, then carefully unscrew the top from one bottle and put a small drop on the back of her left hand. Ask her to lick it slowly to get the taste. Now she chooses a bottle from the second set, unscrews the lid and puts a small drop on the tip of one finger on her right hand. Does it taste the same? No? Set this bottle aside and repeat the process until she finds the match then remove both matching bottles and set them aside.

Your child needs to wash her hands before returning to the remaining bottles and repeating the process. When all four pairs have been matched, she's finished.

CHAPTER
THREE

let me
do it

KEY
IDEA

help me to
do it myself

Independence is the greatest drive of a young child. While working
to achieve it, children have fun practising and mastering many skills.

Stepping out Toddlers get a taste
of independence as they take their
first steps and become mobile.

From very early in life, children want to practise the skills that will make
them independent. Helping children learn to do things for themselves,
from dressing and washing to pouring drinks and making snacks, sets them
on the road to independence.

According to their age, young children can be very helpful around the
house. They can clean up their rooms, help to chop vegetables, sweep up
messes, dust and generally help us in the kitchen as we cook and bake. They
can learn how to set the table, carry food to the table, arrange flowers and
table decorations. They can also learn table manners, how to greet guests at
the door and how to act as nice hosts and hostesses to young friends, guests
and relatives who come to visit. With gentle guidance, children quickly
learn to work neatly, pick up after themselves and help out with chores,
and they will thoroughly enjoy practising these skills.

sense of self Children who feel respected and competent develop
a far greater sense of emotional well-being than children who are doted
upon. The activities in this chapter are designed to help you teach your
child specific everyday living skills that will help him become increasingly
independent and self-confident. Lessons in these skills are intended not

only to teach the skill itself, but also to help your child to develop a sense of calmness, concentration, cooperation, self-discipline and self-reliance. Many have social objectives, too, teaching self-awareness, sensitivity to others and service to the community. Parents have to set the tone and serve as daily role models for everyday living skills. We need to be poised, purposeful, precise, caring and giving.

According to Maria Montessori, "The essence of independence is to be able to do something for one's self. Such experience is not just play. It is work children must do in order to grow up."

life lessons
The lessons your child learns can be broken down into three areas:

- care of himself
- everyday tasks around the house
- grace and courtesy (see chapter four).

Many of these lessons involve the mastery of fine motor skills, such as how to fasten a button, pour from a small jug or carry things without dropping them or stumbling. These are lessons that most parents try to teach their children when they are very young. Hopefully, you will find in this chapter some strategies to help the process go smoothly. They can start at any age, whenever you feel your child is ready. The best way to know when the time is right for each lesson is to pay attention to what your child is telling you, not only with words but with actions. For example, there comes a point when your child will try to hold a cup. That would be the right time to begin teaching him how to drink from it himself.

Gaining independence Your child will reach a point when he is ready and able to do things for himself.

children love to
work and play

Small children want to be part of your world. For them, work is every bit as much fun as play if they are given the chance to do it.

"children need to be shown new skills in simple ways they can understand"

The best way to encourage your child to try new skills is to demonstrate them precisely and slowly in simple ways that he can understand. Then give him time to practise and to be allowed to make his own mistakes and correct them. Try looking at the world from your child's perspective. By giving him clear boundaries and careful guidelines, you can allow him to learn how to do things for himself and give him the self-respect and confidence that come with independence.

a matter of size The first step is to seek out tools and utensils that are the right size for your child. Most of the tasks young children can do are much easier if they have equipment made in a size that is right for their age. It is easy to find child-sized toothbrushes, but there are also child-sized cups, plates, forks, spoons, watering cans, brooms and brushes, and even tubes of toothpaste.

the real thing Why would you buy your child a play kitchen when what she really wants is to be with you helping in the real kitchen? I'm not suggesting that we should turn a three year old loose with a

Setting the table Buy child-sized cutlery. Outlines of each piece show your child how to set the table and where to place her plate and cup.

cleaver or oven, but there are many things that are not dangerous that your child can do if you take the time to teach her how. For example, she can easily stir things that are cool, wash vegetables or learn how to set the table. Children do not always want to do what we are doing, and I am not suggesting that you should make a young child wash the dishes when she really wants to play. But when your child asks or shows that she wants to help, be ready to show her how. And, if you've taken the time to organize your kitchen to provide a small work table and some child-sized basic tools, she is more likely to want to help and to come back again and again.

step by step
Many of the things that we do every day involve several different skills, each of which we learnt along the way. By breaking tasks down into small steps, you can help your child to master each level of difficulty one at a time. Take this approach when you want to teach your child how to sort clean socks in the laundry or put flowers in a vase. Think about each step and how you can make it simple to follow. Explain each step with just a few words as you demonstrate it, so your child concentrates on what you are doing rather than what you are saying. Then let your child practise until she is competent at each stage.

Learning to ride a bicycle is a good step-by-step analogy. When our children are ready, we often give them a tricycle and let them learn how to mount and dismount, how to steer and how to work the pedals. As safe as tricycles are, they usually do not have brakes, and we are careful where we let our children ride them. Eventually the time comes when our children ask for a "big bike". We then choose a bike that is the right size for our child, and it comes equipped with stabilizer wheels. Those extra wheels help keep this much larger bike upright, and allow children to get used to the pedals, steering and brakes. Slowly, they become more and more confident until they ask us to remove the stabilizer wheels. Before we know it, they are zipping around on their bikes, and we are constantly having to remind them to wear their safety helmets!

Step by step, this process of mastering an everyday skill is made easier by careful planning and patient instruction and support from parents. Lessons such as these continue as children grow up. The process of teaching your teenager to drive is a good example of an everyday life skill your child learns when she is almost grown. Learning how to deal with conflicts with friends, manage savings and plan a small party are other examples.

Perhaps one of the most difficult things to do as a parent, once we have taught our children a new skill, is to then allow them to continue to practise this skill as part of their everyday life without interfering. While we would never suggest that a child who has learned to ride a two-wheeler bike goes back to stabilizer wheels, how often do we find ourselves continuing to bundle our children into their coats or shoes long after they are capable of managing to put them on by themselves?

Pedal power Learning to ride a bike is a good example of how we teach our children a new skill step by step.

Learning order Teach your child to take one book off a shelf at a time and to return it when she is finished.

Look at the label Labelling baskets and shelves with photos helps your child return her toys to the right place.

a sense of order

A key element in teaching children everyday life skills is keeping everything tidy. In the crucial sensitive period for order (see page 16), their world needs to be well-organized. If taught where things belong and how to return them correctly when they have finished using them, children internalize this sense of order and carry it with them for the rest of their lives.

Most of us can be overwhelmed by the chaos that quickly develops around the house if we leave things lying around. Children are particularly sensitive to this. Although they are often masters at creating a mess, most find it difficult to clean up after themselves. The most efficient approach is to teach them to clean up as they go along. While some children may be born with a "neat gene", they all can be taught right from the start to work and play in a tidy way without stifling their creativity or stripping playtime of fun.

The secret is to establish a ground rule and gently but firmly teach your child that while she may select anything from her shelves to work and play with for as long as she wishes, she must return it when she is finished with it, and may not remove something new until the last thing has been put away.

Some toys are better when used together with other toys – a set of building blocks and a collection of toy cars, for example. All you need to do in this instance is incorporate the two toys into a collection. Children can easily learn special rules, such as the idea that the toy cars and blocks go together, and it's fine to play with them at the same time. The key idea is to get all of the toy cars and blocks returned to the shelf before your child goes on to the next project.

photographic labels

Use photos on storage containers to help your child return things to the right place. You can also place a photo on each shelf showing how the entire shelf should look when all the toys, games, books and such like that are stored there have been placed back in the proper order. This allows your child to use the photo as a control of error (see page 84) whenever she is returning materials to the shelves after she has finished playing or working with them or inspecting them for damage.

practical storage

As you will recall, I recommend against using toy boxes (see page 37). Set up low shelves to hold your child's books, toys and games in her bedroom and in those rooms around the house where you and the family tend to spend the most time. Find ways to contain toys with many parts to keep them from going everywhere. Usually this involves using some sort of container that is large enough to hold all the pieces and sturdy enough not to fall apart or look tattered with use. Depending on the nature of a particular toy, a heavy plastic container, a strong basket, a sturdy wooden box or perhaps a large jar or bowl provide good solutions.

defined work/play areas

You probably don't want your child finger-painting in the middle of your living-room rug. You certainly don't want her painting on the walls, either. Think about each toy and activity that you are going to make available to your child, and determine where each can be used safely without creating a mess that would be difficult for your child to clean up. Some activities ought to be done in the kitchen or in a room that has a tile floor that makes it fairly simple to clean up spilled food or paint. Some might be fine to use in the family room, but not where people will have to step over them as they come and go. Still others are outdoor activities, such as woodworking or throwing balls, and need to be done in the garden.

Establish your plan, then teach your child how to do things correctly rather than punishing or criticizing her for making mistakes. If you find your child using a toy in the wrong place, redirect her to where this activity belongs. If a mess has been made, it is reasonable, depending on your child's age, to expect her to clean it up or at least to help. This often doesn't work well with toddlers. With them, prevention is the only defence! Don't allow them to get access to something that they should not use.

Some things are fine to work or play with on a sofa. Some are best done at a table. However, children often find that for many of the activities they enjoy they are most comfortable on the floor. Give your child small rugs or mats to define her work/play area. Toys and puzzles have a tendency to spread out all over a room if you don't help your child to contain them. A small rug, perhaps 75 x 120cm (2½ x 4ft), defines an excellent work/play

Roll out the mat Playing on a mat or rug confines activities so pieces don't spread out all over the room.

area on the floor. For larger projects, such as a giant city built of blocks, your child can use two mats together. Teach your child how to roll and unroll her mat and how to store it in a basket.

safe manoeuvres
Think about how your child can safely and carefully carry each toy or utensil from the shelf to where she wants to work and play. Often the best way is for her to carry the toy in its own container. Some toys, games or utensils are easily carried by themselves – a doll, for example. Others involve many pieces and sometimes the set is too large or heavy for a child to carry. In this case, provide small trays that your child can use to carry enough pieces to work with in one or more trips. Keep in mind that children do not automatically know how to carry things on a tray without spilling, so you will need to demonstrate and let your child practise. A small basket may be easier for a child who finds using a tray difficult.

pride of ownership
Teach your child to take care of her toys and other belongings. Rather than punishing her if she breaks something, or simply buying a replacement, take the time to show her how to use things correctly. When a toy, game or anything else is broken, see if it can be repaired, then make that process a lesson itself. Encourage your child to help you repair things and teach her how to do simple repairs herself. Demonstrate how you personally take care of your family home and encourage your children to do likewise on a daily basis. Draw her attention to the small details, such as picking up stray pieces of paper, beads or other debris from the floor.

control of error
Whenever possible, try to build a control of error into each activity so it becomes clear to your child when she has made a mistake. The rationale behind letting children use cups and bowls that break if they are dropped or misused is that children quickly learn to be careful and controlled when they use them. Mistakes are an opportunity for patiently showing your child once more how to do a task correctly, and generally lead to a new lesson in problem solving: "How do we gather up all those beads?" or "How do we safely clean up the broken pieces?"

"when a toy or game is broken, see if it can be repaired, then make that process a lesson itself"

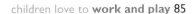

Beautiful toys Children respond
to the beauty of natural materials
such as wood.

beauty and harmony Select toys, tools and other everyday
items that your child will use on the basis of their appropriate size, ease of
handling and beauty. When you choose trays, jugs and other utensils for
your child to use in everyday life skills (see pages 98–105), avoid things
which are cheap and made of plastic – look instead for the most attractive
materials that you can find and afford. Children respond to the beauty of
wood, glass, silver, brass and similar natural materials.

Young children absorb and remember every nuance of their early
home environment. The aim is for you to design activities that will
draw your child's interest and to create prepared surroundings that are
harmonious and beautiful.

getting to grips with
bathroom skills

Learning how to take care of herself – from washing hands to
brushing teeth – will make your child feel confident and capable.

Tap tactics Learning to manage
running water from a tap is a big step
towards bathroom independence.

Many of the skills your child needs to be able to do to look after herself
are learnt in the bathroom. Look carefully at your bathroom and make any
changes needed (see page 41) to ensure this is a safe and comfortable place
for your child to try the following activities.

turning the tap on and off
This is a straightforward task.
It requires a small platform in front of the sink your child uses, allowing her
to get up high enough to use the tap. Be sure a small hand towel is close by
for her to use to dry her hands.

Show your child how to pull out the plug, and explain that it is very
important not to allow the water to overflow from the sink. Show her the
cold water tap, and tell her "This is the tap for cold water." Now show her
the tap for hot water. Tell her "This tap turns on the hot water. You have
to be very careful! The water is so hot that it can hurt you."

Now slowly turn on the cold water, part way, and turn it back off.
Invite your child to turn it on. If she turns it on too fast, say "You have to
be careful not to turn the water on too fast, because it will splash
everywhere." Now ask your child to turn off the tap. Don't be surprised if
she turns the water on full force when she means to turn it off. The point

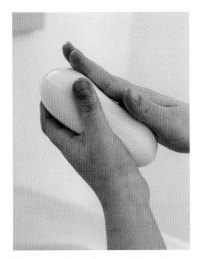

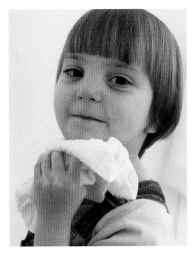

The wonders of soap Although soap doesn't kill germs, it gets them off your child's skin and down the drain.

Clean face Make sure your child has her own flannel and towels at a level she can reach in the bathroom.

of the lesson is to teach her how to control the flow of water in a sink. Repeat the lesson as needed, emphasizing which is the cold water tap and which is the hot, and how to turn the flow on and off.

Once your child can turn the cold water on and off, ask her to try the same thing with the hot water. If you have mixer taps, do this with the cold water flowing first. Explain "If we start the cold water first, and then turn on the hot water, they mix and become warm, but not hot." Show your child how to touch the edge of the water flow lightly to see how hot or cold the water is running. Also show her how to adjust the temperature by turning the hot water tap on more completely or reducing its flow. If you have separate hot and cold taps, you will need to show your child how to run some cold water into the sink with the plug in, then turn the hot water tap and add hot water until the water in the sink is warm.

Now both dry your hands, and you're finished! Don't be surprised if your child wants to practise this exercise over and over again for a while.

washing hands
Once your child understands how to work the tap, introduce the idea of using soap and warm water to wash her hands. In the flu and cold season, germs are most often spread when children

fun with water

Children love to play in water so it is a good idea to set up some place where your child can play safely. You can use the sink, a bowl or a preschool water table set up in a room with a tile floor where spilled water can be easily mopped up.

Establish and enforce some basic ground rules such as no splashing and not allowing certain objects, such as anything sharp or electrical, in or near the water.

Provide some fun things for your child to play with. Good examples include water wheels, boats, a funnel and bottles to fill with water.

Tooth care Buy your child a small toothbrush and teach her to brush her teeth after every meal.

touch their fingers to their eyes, nose or mouth. One of the most effective ways to reduce the spread of infections is to encourage your child to wash her hands often, scrubbing them with soap under the running water for at least 30 seconds. Soap doesn't kill the germs, but it does loosen the dirt and grime. Hand washing under running water in this way is effective because most, if not all, of the germs on your child's hands are washed off and go down the drain. It never hurts to explain why we do things like this, using simple language and a short explanation.

brushing teeth

Once your child knows how to use the sink, brushing her teeth just requires a small toothbrush, pleasant-tasting toothpaste, a mirror and some instruction. Ask your dentist for advice about the best toothbrush and toothpaste to use, as well as the best way to brush, then teach your child to do it in the way your dentist recommends. The general rule is to teach your children to brush after every meal. Don't forget to explain why brushing is so important.

bath time

Many children enjoy the time they spend together with mum or dad at bath time and you will want to supervise until you can clearly see that your child is old enough and capable of bathing herself safely. Usually, sometime between the ages of three and five, your child will let you know that she is old enough to bath herself. Follow her lead, but make sure she knows the correct way to wash her hair and use a face cloth.

brushing hair

Make sure your child has her own brush or comb and show her how to brush and tidy her hair. If she prefers you to brush it for her, that's fine. As she gets older, she might like to learn how to put in easy-to-use hair clips and bands.

Tidy hair Having her own hairbrush or comb helps your child to learn to take pride in her appearance.

Quick to learn Set up a small station in the bathroom for your child so all the things she needs are in easy reach.

introducing toileting

Children learn to use the toilet when they are ready, not when their parents get around to training them. Readiness to use the toilet, rather than wearing nappies, depends largely on the maturation of a child's nervous system, as well as the desire to feel independent and grown up. This tends to vary from one child to another. You cannot hurry the process, and gentle patience is certainly a virtue. But, like so many aspects of living with children, if we understand how things develop, we can prepare the environment and play a supporting role.

It all revolves around your child's amazing brain and nervous system. When children are born, their brains and nervous systems are at an incomplete stage of development. Between birth and 18 months, the cells of the nervous system become coated with myelin, a fatty substance which facilitates the transmission of impulses from cell to cell more efficiently throughout the nervous system. This allows babies and toddlers to gain more and more refined control and coordination of their movements.

This process of myelinization, or integration of the nervous system, develops in stages. Babies gain control of their head, then arms and the trunk of their body and eventually legs and feet. From random movements, they gain the ability to move with conscious intent and control.

toilet curiosity

Children often become interested in toilets when they are about a year old. They like to flush and often want to play with the water in them. If this is the case with your child, give him access to more appropriate water play, such as water in the bathroom sink. About this time, children also become fascinated with their "poo" and "wee". Don't be surprised or offended. Just explain that "Everyone poos – it is how our bodies get rid of the part of what we eat that we cannot use."

By 15 months, many children become interested in dressing and undressing themselves. They often also express interest in wearing pants and may try on their older siblings' or parents'. This is probably an indication that they are becoming curious about learning to use the toilet.

Around 18 months, children enter a sensitive period in which they can most easily gain control of their now much more developed and integrated nervous system. At this stage most children have both the

toileting tips

- **Be patient** and encouraging.
- **Prepare your bathroom** to support your child's independence.
- **Dress your child in cotton training pants** during the day.
- **Teach your child how to undress**, clean up, flush and dress again step by step, when he seems ready to start using the toilet.
- **Explain bodily functions** patiently.
- **Keep old towels on hand** so your child can clean up accidents.
- **When accidents occur,** be gently understanding.

physical ability and the interest to control bladder and bowel. If they are given the opportunity to spend as much time as possible in pants, rather than nappies, they gain a greater awareness of these bodily functions.

like a big boy

A young child's nervous system is now much more developed and capable of recognizing physical sensations and controlling the bladder and sphincter muscles. If you dress your child in cotton pants rather than nappies at this stage, at least during the day, he will have the occasional accident, but he will also become acutely aware of it. Children wearing disposable nappies can rarely sense that they have had a wee. Wearing pants, they are much more likely to learn to recognize the sensation when their bladder is full and tend to take pride in using the toilet like a big boy or girl.

About now, many children will want to sit on the toilet or potty in imitation of their parents and older siblings, even though they have not yet developed bladder and bowel control. Gently support your child's interest, slowly teaching him how to pull down his pants, sit on the toilet correctly, use toilet paper to wipe his bottom, pull his pants up, flush the toilet and wash his hands.

Be prepared for occasional accidents. When they occur, stay calm and be reassuring. Keep clean pants on hand where your child can get to them and set up a stack of old towels that he can use to wipe up accidents. Help your child when he requests it or if he is clearly overwhelmed, but don't rush in and make him feel ashamed.

Learning to use the toilet is a natural process that begins when your child's desire to be grown up and his neurological development have reached the point where he can control his bladder and bowels. We don't train children to use the toilet, we support them when they are ready.

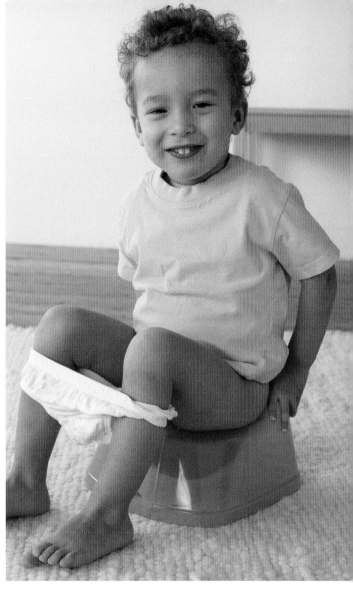

I can do it Using the potty is a natural process that grows out of neurological development and the drive for independence.

ACTIVITY
FOCUS

Complete mastery Give
your child time to practise, and
she will soon master even the
more complicated fastenings.

the art of getting
dressed

In no time at all, your child will be undressing
and dressing herself at a moment's notice.

Somewhere between the ages of six months and a year, most children begin to hold out a hand or foot while they are being dressed. At about 18 months, many toddlers want to start wearing pants like their older siblings or friends (see pages 90–1). Some may begin to take delight in dressing and undressing themselves and it is not uncommon for children of this age to try on their older siblings' or parents' clothing. These are all signs that your child is ready to start dressing herself.

When your toddler starts to show an interest, make time for some trying-on sessions with hats, scarves and slippers. Sit on the floor next to your child and both put on trousers together, then socks and a T-shirt. Make your careful demonstration into a game.

everything within reach You will remember when I was
describing how to organize your child's bedroom (see pages 41–3) I talked about the importance of providing hooks, hangers, shelves and baskets that are low enough so that your child can reach them on her own, and drawers that she can easily open herself. Take a close look at her bedroom and make sure everything is accessible.

practise first

Encourage your child to practise dressing skills before trying them out on clothes she is wearing.

Fastening buttons Allow her to practise buttoning and unbuttoning on a piece of clothing with large buttons laid on the floor.

Bow-tying frame This has two different-coloured ribbons, one attached to each side, to help master the skill of tying bows.

I can dress myself! At about 18 months your child may start to develop an interest in putting her clothes on by herself.

As children get older and more independent, it is a good idea to give them choices. Set out two outfits that your child can choose from each morning. As the day draws to a close, discuss with her which clothes she might like to wear the following morning. You can also help by buying clothing that is easy for your toddler or young child to put on and take off by herself. Look for trousers with elastic waistbands, rather than belts. Avoid clothes that have lots of buttons or zips until your child is ready to enjoy the challenge. Choose shoes that slip on or fasten with Velcro. Try to be patient as your child learns to dress herself. Young children need lots of practice.

GETTING READY Putting on simple items such as a hat and a scarf is a good starting point when your child is ready to master the skills he needs to dress himself.

SOCKS ON Managing to put on his own socks will require manual dexterity from your child. Show him how to get them the right way round and pull them on.

VELCRO SHOES Shoes with Velcro fasteners are the easiest for young children to learn with once they are ready to start putting their shoes on by themselves.

TYING LACES Learning to tie shoe laces usually takes a lot of practice to perfect. A bow-tying frame (see facing page) is useful when your child starts learning this skill.

step by step: putting on a coat

ONE Eden lays his coat on the floor with the lining uppermost and squats down at the top where the hood is.

TWO Slotting his hands into the sleeves, he lifts the coat over his head. The sleeves slide down over his arms.

THREE The coat falls neatly down over his back and Eden straightens out the front. "See, I can do it myself!"

Putting on a coat can be the most awkward aspect of getting dressed for a young child. From time to time even adults struggle to find a sleeve left hanging somewhere behind. In Montessori nurseries in winter when a large group of small children all need to put on coats at the same time to go outside, there is a simple technique they are taught to help them get ready with the minimum of assistance. This technique is just as easy to learn and use at home.

preparation helps Start by organizing your hall with shoe racks and a low peg on which your child can hang his coat (see page 41). Show your child how to pull his coat sleeves the right way out each time he hangs it up. Now show him how to put on his coat following the steps in the sequence above. Approaching the coat from the collar end is important (many children end up with an upside down coat the first few times) so demonstrate this step carefully. When your child masters this trick he will feel a huge sense of independence and achievement, so let him practise as much as he wants to.

FOUR Having practised to perfection, Eden can now put on his coat all by himself in less than 30 seconds. He beams with pride.

shoe order

Pegging pairs of shoes and boots together helps your child to find them easily and presents her with right and left in their proper order when she is ready to put them on.

helping out around the house

Children naturally want to be with us around the house when they are young. Most want to help, if only to feel useful and more grown up.

"think of household chores as a family activity in which children can participate"

If you think of the household chores as a family activity in which children are welcome to participate even when they are very young, you can instill in your children a sense of pride in keeping the house and garden neat and clean. Work should never be thought of as a chore, but as an activity that leads to a sense of order and completion.

Obviously, children do not know how to do everything that we can do, and it often seems easier simply to do things yourself. But by taking the time to prepare the environment and to teach children patiently how to do things step by step, you continue the process of teaching skills as well as attitudes about work.

the right approach Start by gathering together equipment that will enable your child to help. She will need a child-sized broom, mop and bucket, and her own feather duster, cleaning cloths and access to the polishes and other cleaning supplies that you use. She also needs a way to reach some of the areas where she most wants to help, such as the kitchen sink, but is not yet tall enough to reach.

Remember that whereas adults do their chores without thinking about the process, children need to have complex tasks broken down into

step by step: sweeping up

ONE A taped square on the kitchen floor gives Catherine a target towards which she can sweep debris.

TWO Having learnt how to hold her broom with both hands, she carefully sweeps the bits into the square.

THREE To finish, Catherine uses a dust pan and brush to pick up the sweepings. She holds the dust pan level and gets up carefully, watching it all the time as she carries it to the rubbish bin.

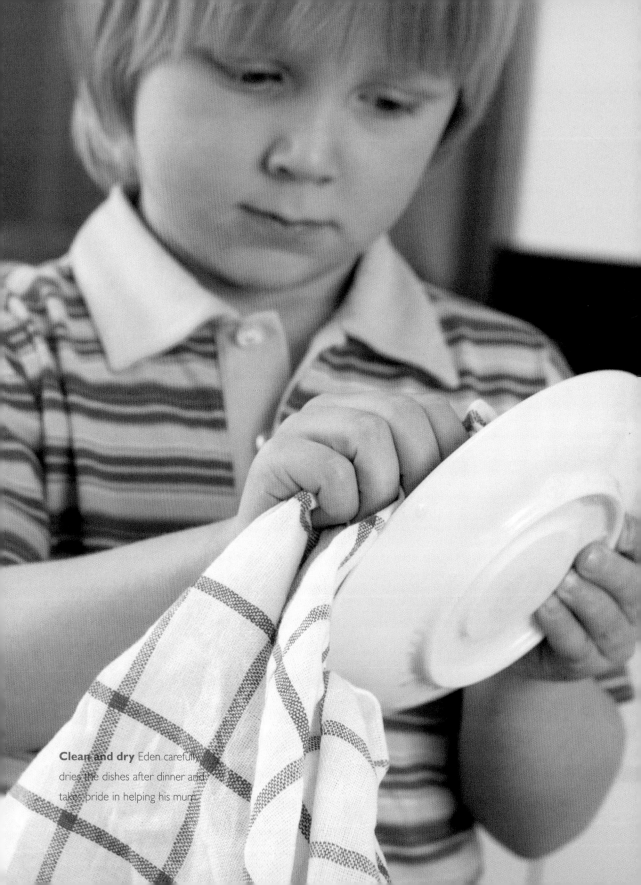

Clean and dry Eden carefully dries the dishes after dinner and takes pride in helping his mum.

your little helpers

Fun with water Lily-Rose loves to do the washing up – it's as much fun as water play but with real responsibility.

Shoe shining Polishing shoes gives Luc a sense of achievement that stays with him whenever he looks at them.

Dustbuster Using the feather duster to help his mum with the housework is one of Fred's favourite activities.

small steps. While your child is learning a skill, it's important to ritualize these steps, making sure that everything is done using the same equipment each time and in the same order. Children learn by practice and repetition. Don't be surprised if your child does something over and over for weeks or months until she has mastered the skill.

Of course, it is not the aim to turn your child into a little slave. You should assume that sometimes she will be anxious to help, and at other times she will be engrossed in another activity. The draw to help out will usually be her desire for your attention and approval. Young children will probably not want to go off on their own to accomplish a task. Instead, your child will be more likely to follow you around and will want to help with the job in which you are engaged. If you approach things correctly, without nagging, impatience, criticism and redoing something your child has done because it is not quite perfect, she will take delight in helping to care for her home.

Pouring lentils Lily-Rose practises pouring lentils from one jug to another. A coloured tray catches any that spill.

Water skills Supporting the jug with both hands, Lily-Rose then practises using water instead of lentils.

learning to pour
Learning to pour liquids is much easier to master if you give your child small jugs with handles that are the right size for her small hands, and which are not too heavy for her to control when they are full. The entire process is also made easier if as a first step you teach your child how to pour something dry, such as uncooked rice or lentils, from one small jug to another. For this first exercise, very small jugs such as those used for cream are the best size. It is a good idea to put a coloured tray under the jugs, then any spilled rice or lentils will be contained and can be easily seen and cleaned up when your child has finished practising.

Show your child how to grasp the handle of the jug using whichever hand she is most comfortable with. Then demonstrate how to support the jug just under the spout with her other hand. This gives her maximum control as she pours. The exercise is to pour the dry rice or lentils from one jug into the other. When done, she can repeat the process with the other jug. Emphasize to your child the importance of being careful. "Darling, see if you can pour the rice from one jug to the other without spilling a single grain of rice."

An independent step Lily-Rose is now able to pour water carefully without spilling and can pour herself a drink whenever she is thirsty.

When your child has mastered this task, you can make it more challenging for her by giving her slightly larger jugs, and then by having her try to pour the rice from the jug into a glass. You can make it more likely that your child will succeed by not putting more rice into the jug than the glass will hold. Finally, when you think your child is ready, place water instead of dried rice in the jug. Challenge her to pour the water into the glass without spilling a drop.

Remember, this process is not learnt in a day! It takes most young children many months of practice to gain the hand-eye coordination needed to pour correctly without any help.

spooning food

While all of us try to teach our children good table manners, part of the process involves helping them to gain enough fine muscle control so that they are at least physically capable of getting food from a plate to their mouths without dropping it.

Trying some practice games with bowls, spoons and forks will help to develop mealtime skills. Start with a tray and two bowls, one of which contains something fairly easy to spoon, such as dried butter beans. You will need a spoon that is the right size for your child. Show her how to transfer the beans, one at a time, from one bowl to the other. Challenge your child to do it herself. When she has finished, she can repeat the process as many times as she wants.

Once she can do this without spilling, increase the level of difficulty by replacing the large butter beans with something more challenging, such as dried rice. Repeat the process.

You can use the same process for teaching your child to use a fork if you select the right substances to transfer, such as cubes of cheese or cooked green peas.

Knife skills Begin by teaching your child how to use a knife to cut up something soft such as a banana.

Snack attack Tom has been shown how to spread cream cheese on a cracker to make a snack.

Slicing banana He neatly slices some banana on a chopping board and adds it to his snack.

Ready to go Tom has learnt how to pour from his own little jug of juice. Now his snack is complete.

preparing a snack One way to encourage your child to eat healthy snacks is to get him involved in making them himself. Begin by teaching your child how to use a small knife. Choose one that has a rounded point, such as a small cheese knife. This type of knife has an edge just sharp enough to cut through soft cheese or a banana. Show your child how to grip the handle correctly and how to use it to spread butter, jam and such like on a cracker.

Once he has mastered spreading, you can go on to teach your child how to use the knife to cut up soft food, such as a banana. As he gets older, stronger and more able to control the knife, give him more difficult things to slice, such as carrots and celery.

Make sure your child can easily reach all the ingredients and utensils he needs to make a snack without help. Items that need to be stored in the fridge should be kept on a low shelf comfortably within his reach.

Once your child is confident preparing a snack for himself, encourage him to prepare a plate of sliced banana and some crackers spread with butter or margarine and jam. Add some toothpicks that can be used to lift the slices of banana from the plate and suggest he offers the food to everyone in the family.

CHAPTER FOUR

keeping the peace

KEY
IDEA

create a
loving climate

We can help our children to learn good behaviour, courtesy and compassion by demonstration, reassurance and unconditional love.

Making an impression Happy times spent with you leave a lasting impression in your baby's memory.

In a Montessori–inspired home, parents try to be empathetic and caring, respecting children as real and separate human beings. Children also need to develop a sense of empathy for others, and must learn the rules of courteous everyday behaviour. To accomplish this, we need to help them learn self-respect as well as compassion and respect for others. Since we cannot always be with them, we need to teach them to act with honour and integrity whether or not someone is watching. We can't prepare them for every situation that they will face over the years, but we can teach them how to apply general rules of kind behaviour to new situations.

baby behaviour
Babies and toddlers don't respond to discipline, rules and punishments, but they do respond to unconditional love. They are not yet at a stage where they know right from wrong. They live in the moment, and when they want something, they want it "right now".

One secret of living happily with very young children is to work hard at understanding what they are trying to communicate when they cry. Crying is one of the few ways they can communicate. It can mean that they are hungry or that they need to be winded, they may be in an uncomfortable position or they may need a nappy change.

Remember, babies are people, too! They can become frightened. They may be bored or lonely. They can have bad dreams. Watch and listen carefully. If you pay attention to your child, ultimately you will be able to determine what she is trying to tell you. The behaviour of babies and toddlers is impulse driven and they have a limited ability even to make the choice to follow ground rules. While you always want to model good behaviour and explain why a given behaviour is acceptable, or not, don't be surprised when your words go unheeded.

In a climate of love and respect, toddlers develop the ability to understand our words and will begin consciously to respond to them. Eventually, they imitate our actions when we model polite behaviour and will begin to cooperate. Most toddlers have good days when they are cooperative and angelic, and not so good days where they seem to be testing us constantly.

Parent teacher As parents we must teach our children how to cope with and express their emotions.

teaching older children Our children love us with a profound affection and want us to be pleased with them. Our aim is to take our children beyond simple obedience, where they do what we ask in hope of a reward or to avoid something unpleasant. Ultimately, we want to help them to develop an internalized sense of polite, caring behaviour and of what is right and wrong. This requires that children develop a social conscience and a sense of self-discipline, which can only happen as they slowly mature.

Children have the same emotions as adults, but they don't instinctively know how to express frustration and anger appropriately, nor do they automatically know how to solve conflicts. As parents, we have to teach our children how to get along with other people, so that they are kind and courteous even when we aren't present. For better or worse, all parents are moral educators. Our goal is to show our children the values we hold dear, and to teach them in such a way that they live by them. Children who achieve this develop a high level of self-respect. They also tend to find it easier to establish strong friendships. They respect the rights of others, and are generally pleasant to be around.

As your child gets older, don't take it for granted that he will automatically know how to handle a new situation. It is always better to teach him the right way to act than to wait for him to misbehave and then scold, threaten or punish him. If your child does act inappropriately, stop his misbehaviour calmly, but firmly, then show him how to handle the situation in a socially acceptable way.

"it's better to teach your child the right way to act than to wait for him to misbehave, then scold, threaten or punish him"

the importance of respect Some parents and teachers believe that they can shape a child's personality and future through strict discipline. But children carry within themselves the key to their own development. Their early attempts to express their individuality are hesitant and tentative. Our goal should be to help our children to become mature, independent and responsible. Unfortunately, as parents, we sometimes overprotect our children, not realizing that they can only learn about life through experience, just as we did.

We want to help our children learn to live in peace and harmony with themselves, with all people and with the environment. We work to create a home in which they can learn to function as independent, thinking people. To succeed, we need to treat them with respect as full and complete human beings, who happen to be in our care. Our children need to feel that it is fine to be themselves. If they believe that they are not living up to our expectations or that we are disappointed in the people that they are becoming, then there is a good chance that their lives will be emotionally scarred.

sidestepping
tantrums

During tantrums, both children and parents can get completely out of control – but one of you has to be the grown-up.

"a tantrum may be your child's way of testing the limits to see how you will react"

Temper tantrums are typical among toddlers, although some children carry them on for many years if they find they are a way of getting what they want. Children most commonly throw a tantrum because they are extremely tired, irritably hungry, emotionally overwhelmed or feeling sick. As your child becomes more "knowing", tantrums may be no more than her way of testing the limits or seeing how you will react.

Children always pick the worst possible times to throw tantrums. You may be driving your car, out shopping, eating at a restaurant or at a friend's house, and just when you would least expect your child to make a scene, she does. Our tendency is to want to do something right away to get her to stop. We are embarrassed and our stress level soars. This is when parents often resort to threats and punishments. Instead, we need to remember that the tantrum means something, and the only thing that works is to get to the bottom of it and try to address our child's needs.

types of tantrum
There is a real difference between a temper tantrum in a child who is tired, hungry or sick, and one thrown by a child who is angry, frustrated and testing the limits. The first type of tantrum requires little more than a parent determining the cause, remaining calm

and upbeat, and helping with food and rest, reassurance and comfort. While it can be embarrassing to have a child crying uncontrollably in a supermarket or on a social outing, at least there is a physical situation underlying the tantrum that can be resolved once you figure it out. If you do your best to be in control, eventually you will be.

The second type of tantrum is like any power struggle. It is your child's less than articulate way of trying to assert some control in a situation where she feels powerless. Remember, whenever children say "No!" or have a temper tantrum, they are trying to communicate something to you. You have to stay calm, step back and try to determine what the hidden message is. It might be that all that's needed is for you to listen. Just like adults, children sometimes simply don't feel that anyone is listening to them.

Cause and effect Your child may throw a temper tantrum because she is tired, hungry or sick.

behaviour patterns

Often there are patterns in family life. See if you can identify triggers for tantrums, then avoid them.

• **Leave your child with a sitter** if she tends to have tantrums when you go shopping.

• **Talk plans through** with your child in advance and stick to them – children often play up when plans change abruptly.

• **Explain the limits to your child** before you do something. For example, if you are going to the shops and your child wants to buy a toy, tell her in advance what you will agree to and stick to it.

You choose Avoid power struggles by giving your child choices. For example, choose two outfits you are happy for her to wear then ask her to choose the one she prefers – this way she still feels she has some control.

resolving issues

It may be difficult sometimes to know for sure what a temper tantrum is all about because your child is not capable of explaining the problem. However, most parents learn to recognize symptoms and can make an educated guess.

• If you believe your child's behaviour is a result of her being hungry, find some food for her to eat as soon as possible, even if it's not her usual mealtime. It's always a good idea to carry some sort of healthy snack with you for just such emergencies.

• If you believe that your child is overly tired, minimize your talking and speak in a soothing voice, hold or rock her, and take her to her bedroom or some place where she can rest as soon as possible.

• If you believe that your child is ill, speak in a soothing voice, quietly reassuring her. If you think she is going to be sick, see if someone nearby can get you an empty bowl or rubbish bin and a warm facecloth. If she needs medical attention, make the arrangements as calmly as possible.

• Some children have a hard time with transitions, and this in itself can lead to a tantrum. For example, if you are at the playground, let your child know in advance that you will be leaving soon. "We'll have to go home in 10 minutes. Would you like to go down the slide again or go on the swing?" The reminder in advance and the choice will help your child to manage transitions more smoothly.

• If your child is clearly testing the limits, stay calm and avoid getting into an argument. Speak in a soothing voice, gently letting her know that while you understand that she is angry, this is still the rule. For example, "I know that you wish you could stay here at the playground, but we have to get home to make lunch."

• If you have been talking to a friend for a long time at the lunch table or on the phone make sure you give your toddler plenty of attention when you have finished.

Do not give in to children's attempts to get you to back down, whether they are whining, demanding or attempting to manipulate the situation. Distracting a toddler with a game at the first sign of a tantrum can work. However, if she does not calm down, you probably ought to disengage either by sitting down to read or by leaving the room. Obviously, you wouldn't do that if you suspect that she will do something truly dangerous.

don't overload
Many families try to do too much. Remember, toddlers prefer fixed routines and get angry and tired when swept along from one activity to the next. Sometimes it is unavoidable, but think long and hard before you sign your child up for dance lessons, baby gym or any other prescheduled classes for young children. Racing from one activity to another raises everyone's stress levels and sets the stage for temper tantrums. Allow enough time so that you will not have to race to meet a deadline.

coping tips

There are several things that you should remember when your child is having a tantrum:

• **Don't resort to violence** by slapping or spanking your child. That is the surest way to teach her to be violent to others.

• **Don't try to restrain your child physically** in the midst of a temper tantrum, unless she is about to run out into traffic or harm herself in some other very real and immediate way.

• **Don't resort to threats or punishments**. When children are being irrational, these simply don't work and only escalate the emotional turmoil already begun.

• **Don't argue**. You can't win a debate with someone who is being irrational!

• **Don't try to embarrass your child** or ridicule her behaviour. This teaches her to lash out at other people in the future.

• **Don't attempt to deal with a temper tantrum in public**. Take your child to somewhere you can be alone and talk in private. This is courteous to the people around you, and makes it easier for you to handle the situation.

banishing bedtime battles

Bedtime can either be a special time or turn into a power struggle between parents and children. Children can resist going to sleep for many reasons: they resent being told they have to; they are afraid that they will miss something; they are not tired; or they simply want to remain close to their parents. As in any situation, ask yourself what your child's behaviour is really trying to tell you. Then look for a way to give your child some of what she wants, and still get her to go to bed.

establish a routine A good bedtime routine might include a bedtime snack, followed by a bath, brushing of teeth, reading a story, then a snuggle before tucking your child in and kissing her goodnight. Do the same thing every evening; bedtime rituals help children to calm down and feel reassured.

Begin your bedtime ritual an hour or so before you actually hope to have your child asleep. Keep everything calm. This is not the time to do anything to encourage excitement. Give a warning 10 minutes or so before it will be time to begin the ritual. This allows your child time to wind up whatever activities she is engaged in. Try to avoid power struggles by offering your child choices, each of which is acceptable in your eyes. For example, "Would you like Mummy or Daddy to tuck you in tonight?"

If your child has difficulty going to sleep, try using guided visualization. This is a process where you use words to describe a pleasant, calming experience. Some parents use soothing music in the background. You might tell a gentle story, such as how you and your child are going on a trip by magic carpet or sailing down a beautiful river.

Another strategy parents use is to have a conversation with their child about happy memories. "Do you remember when you were little and I used to carry you on my shoulders?" Or you might tell each other something that you particularly appreciate about one another: "I love the way you are so kind to everyone. It makes me really proud to be your Mum." You can encourage your child to talk about her day by asking the right questions in the right way. For example, "What was the best thing about today?" rather than "What did you do today?", which usually prompts the answer "Nothing."

"do the same thing every evening; bedtime rituals help children to calm down and feel reassured"

be consistent

Once your bedtime ritual is done, leave your child's bedroom quietly. To avoid the endless pattern of your child getting up and coming to find you, tell her in advance that "Except for a real emergency, if you come to find me after you've gone to bed, I will gently take you back to your room." Don't get into a debate, and don't give in. Be calm, gentle and consistent. Consistency is important, because if you are inconsistent your child will bend the rules more and more to see if they still hold true. But don't be too rigid – sometimes the rules have to be set aside to respond to something important that is going on with your child. For example, she may wake up in the middle of the night and need to be with you because she is frightened or sick. Follow your instincts.

Bedtime ritual Reading a story is a useful calming activity as your child winds down towards going to sleep.

positive approach
to discipline

Many parents believe that the word discipline
means to punish. In reality, it means to teach.

Direct action Make it one of your
ground rules that your child cleans
up himself if he spills something.

Every child will test the rules to some degree. In fact, most acts of testing
parents are a normal part of a child's process of growing up. When children
test adults, it is often their way of expressing feelings that they don't
understand, and from our responses they gradually learn how to handle
their emotions appropriately. By testing the limits, they learn that we really
care about certain ground rules of grace and courtesy in our relationships.
In acting out, they are taking their first tentative steps towards independence,
attempting to demonstrate that we don't control them completely.

family ground rules
Agree on your family ground rules and
get them written down and displayed where both parents can refer to
them. Teach your child how to do the right thing rather than focusing on
his mistakes. In the Montessori-inspired home there are usually just a
few basic rules:

- Treat everyone with respect.
- If you use something, put it back correctly when you are finished.
- If you break or spill something, clean it up.
- Tell the truth and don't be afraid to admit when you make a mistake.

You should be absolutely clear in your mind about your family ground

rules. Explain them positively, rather than as prohibitions. Instead of saying "Don't do that!" the rules should tell your child what he should do. Teach him how to follow them as if you were teaching any lesson in everyday living skills. Model the same behaviours that you are trying to encourage in your children. Consciously try to catch your child doing something right – reinforce and acknowledge even small steps in the right direction. Don't wait until he has mastered every new skill, encourage him along the way.

When your child is breaking a ground rule, there are several things you can do other than scold, threaten or punish. You can redirect him by

Teaching tidiness Show your child how to put his toys away after he has finished playing with them.

Broken rules If one of your ground rules is no climbing on the furniture yet you find your children bouncing on the sofa, politely but firmly ask them to stop, then remind them of the rule and why you have it.

suggesting a more appropriate choice. You can remind him of the ground rule and politely but firmly ask him to stop. If the situation is not emotionally charged (that is, if you are not personally aggravated), you can re-teach the basic lesson about how to handle such situations.

Be consistent. If you can't bring yourself to reinforce a rule again and again, it shouldn't be a ground rule in your house. A few good rules are much better than dozens of rules that are often ignored.

cut down on "no"
Sooner or later, every child will stubbornly say "No, I don't want to!" This is the classic power struggle that starts in the toddler years and often continues throughout childhood and adolescence. Many people call the toddler stage the "terrible twos!" But it doesn't have to be – not with two year olds or with older children (see panel right).

Power struggles get going in situations where parents and children are each determined to get their own way, and neither party is willing to back down. Underneath, each feels frustrated and threatened. Parents feel that their children are directly challenging their authority. Children in situations such as this are usually feeling powerless, and are attempting to assert their autonomy and establish more of a balance of power in their relationship with their parents.

don't punish, teach
Threats and punishments are not good tools to get children to behave. When children are angry, or are asserting their independence, they often misbehave and don't care if they are punished. On the other hand, children who respond to threats and are shaken by punishments are anxious to please us and win back our love. Arguably, these children will respond just as well to other forms of discipline. While punishments tend to produce immediate results, they are rarely long-lasting and work only if the person being threatened cares.

Teach your child to do things correctly and emphasize the positive rather than using insults and anger. It's not always easy. Above all else, try never to ask your child unanswerable questions, such as, "How many times do I have to tell you ...?" to which the appropriate response would be, "I don't know, Dad! How many times do you have to tell me?" If you ask a silly question, you're likely to get a silly answer.

"no" strategies

Here are some strategies to help reduce the number of power struggles and use of "No!"

• **Give your child choices.** Whenever you can, look for ways to let your child make a choice between two equally acceptable alternatives. "Would you like water or tomato juice with dinner?"

• **Teach your child to say "no" politely.** "Mum, I really do not feel like doing that now."

• **Remember Robert Heinlein's golden rule of family life:** "Kindness and courtesy are even more important between husbands and wives, and parents and children, than between total strangers."

• **Don't simply give in.** Look for ways that might allow you to back down gracefully. Often, through compromise, both you and your child can get most, if not all, of what you are after.

• **Power struggles can be minimized** by giving your child meaningful levels of independence and responsibility. This makes her feel powerful and grown up.

• **Reserve "no"** for the really important issues such as an activity that might harm your child or others or cause damage.

teaching lessons in
grace and courtesy

Practising with games that teach good manners can help
your child learn how to behave well in any company.

Lend a hand Being helpful to
younger children is a key lesson
in grace and courtesy.

Few people seem to consider the value of teaching children the fine
details of acceptable behaviour. In Montessori schools the "lessons in grace
and courtesy" – exercises which set a tone of respect and kindness – sit
alongside the more conventional subjects on the curriculum. We show
our children how to shake hands, greet a friend and say goodbye. We
demonstrate how to interrupt someone who is busy and how to tell
someone "no thank you" politely. We teach children how to speak indoors
and how to play nicely. We show them how to offer a sincere apology and
how to resolve conflicts peacefully.

simple lessons
The first step is to explain a situation in simple
terms and demonstrate the right way to handle it. Then have your child
practise with you, role playing the sequence of events. Children enjoy
these lessons so long as they are kept short, and if they have not been
embarrassed or threatened for making a mistake.

For example, if your child tends to yell at the top of her lungs inside
the house, you need to show her how to keep the noise to a level that
does not disturb other people. First, as it is happening, instead of scolding,
politely but firmly ask your child to speak softly please. Then, choose a

Telephone manners
Mia knows how to answer the telephone politely, listen carefully, then share her news.

courtesy lessons

Here are some more ideas for lessons in grace and courtesy:

• saying "please" and "thank you"

• using a kind tone when speaking: no whining or yelling

• how to ask for a turn or if you can play, too

• how to introduce yourself

• how to open and close doors

• what to do if you have to cough or sneeze

• giving people compliments and encouragement

• allowing others to pass in front of you or to go first

• saying "excuse me" if you bump into someone

• responding politely when someone calls you or says your name

• walking around areas where other children are working or playing on the floor and not stepping over them

• learning how to wait

• not interrupting other people when they are talking

• answering the telephone politely

moment when neither you nor your child are upset about the behaviour to give her the lesson on the right way to speak indoors. Speak in simple language and show her what you mean. For example, you might say: "I want to talk to you about indoor voices. When we are outdoors, it's so big, and sometimes we need to shout so we can hear each other. Outdoors, it doesn't hurt our ears when someone talks loudly. So outdoors we can use our outdoor voices. But when we are indoors, it hurts our ears and bothers the neighbours, too, if we talk too loud. Indoors, we need to use our indoor voices."

Now show your child what you mean. Talk very loud, and ask, "Was I using my indoor voice or my outdoor voice?" Talk normally. "What do you think? Was I using my indoor or my outdoor voice? Indoors, we use our indoor voices. Outdoors, we use our outdoor voices."

You can teach all sorts of lessons this way, such as saying "please" and "thank you" or closing doors without slamming. Some families have the manner of the week. They introduce a new rule of everyday courtesy each week, and practise it with one another over meals and around the house.

role models

To teach children good manners, they need to see that their parents, older siblings and friends follow them consistently as well. The example that we set through our own behaviour is more powerful than anything we say. Children are absorbing everything they see us do, especially when they are very young, and soon they begin to talk and act just like us. We are their role models.

Bearing in mind that your child will be influenced profoundly by the people around her, choose wisely the children and adults with whom your child will spend time. Avoid loud, chaotic situations where large groups of children are over-stimulated and generally behave rudely.

Choose your child's playmates thoughtfully. If she spends time with a family that allows children to create havoc in their home, don't be surprised when your child brings that behaviour home with her. Pay attention to the way prospective playmate's parents supervise their children. Do they ignore them or talk on the phone amidst chaos? It is not your place to judge other families and how they behave, but it is your obligation to make good choices for your child.

learning kindness, courtesy and manners

MEET AND GREET Teach your child the correct way to welcome visitors into his home.

CARE AND COMPASSION Encourage your child to show concern for a friend who is upset.

TABLE MANNERS Your child can learn to pull a chair out and put it back, and how to sit down on it correctly.

COORDINATION AND CONTROL Practising walking carefully along a line, watching where she is going, teaches your child balance and coordination.

CAREFUL CARRYING Teach your child how to bring something to you, carrying it using both hands, and then to set it down correctly.

SAYING GOODBYE Your child starts to learn friendship skills when she is shown how to offer warm greetings and goodbyes.

ACTIVITY
FOCUS

solving problems at the
peace table

When children need help to resolve issues
themselves, direct them to the peace table.

From time to time, children fall out with siblings or friends – it may be
over something as simple as whose turn it is to play with a toy or over a
bigger issue such as friendships. Sometimes they reach the point where
they are too angry to reason with each other. This is where the peace table
comes in, providing a place where the children can cool off as they follow
a procedure that stops the argument in its tracks.

The peace table is usually a child-sized table with two chairs, a bell
and a flower or ornament that symbolizes peace, perhaps a rose, an olive
twig or a dove. If you're short of space, two chairs together are fine or a rug
in the corner of a room or even a particular spot on the stairs. When children
are accustomed to the ritual they may go to the peace table without being
prompted; at other times a parent or older sibling may see a row developing
and suggest the participants try to solve their problem at the peace table.

Once at the table, a certain procedure ensues. The child who feels
especially wronged places one hand on the table and her other hand on
her heart, indicating that she speaks the truth, from the heart. She then
looks at the other child, speaks her name and explains how she feels about
what has occurred and how she would like the disagreement to be settled.

Peace and harmony The peace table helps teach children how to maintain a harmonious and cooperative environment.

Coping with conflict It started with a tussle for a toy, but now Gemma and Tom are beginning to hurt each other and are not able to listen to reason.

The second child then has a turn and the dialogue continues until an agreement is reached. If the children cannot manage this themselves, they may need a mediator – maybe an older sibling or a parent. If the problem is too involved, they may ask for a family council, where the whole family listens to both sides of the story.

What children learn from the peace table is that regardless of their size, age or position in the family, their point of view will be heard and they can expect to be treated fairly. The core experience they gain from these procedures is that arguments need to be settled with honesty and good will to maintain a harmonious, cooperative atmosphere at home.

TIME TO TALK In an effort to resolve their dispute, Gemma and Tom each take a seat at the peace table.

TOM'S TURN Tom puts one hand on the peace table and his other hand on his heart and calmly explains to Gemma what it is about her behaviour that is upsetting him.

NEXT IT'S GEMMA'S TURN Gemma now proceeds in the same way, placing one hand on the table and the other on her heart, and responds to what Tom has said.

IN AGREEMENT When both Gemma and Tom feel that the differences between them are resolved, they ring a bell together to let the rest of the family know.

taking control of
the television

Television is a major source of conflict in many households. Establish some family ground rules regarding viewing, then stick to them.

Hypnotic viewing Children will sit passively for hours in front of a TV set when allowed to do so.

Children's values and knowledge about the world have traditionally been shaped by four cultural influences: home, school, religious organizations and peer groups. Today, television represents a fifth and incredibly powerful culture over which most of us have scant knowledge and exercise little control. This is unfortunate, especially when you consider that it has become the babysitter of choice in all too many families.

passive parents There are several problems with uncontrolled television and children. The violence portrayed is of great concern. In one year a child might see thousands of murders, fights, car crashes and mid-air explosions. Certainly, the values and problem-solving approaches considered appropriate by many producers differ from our own.

An even greater concern is the hypnotic character of television viewing. Many parents observe that their young children can sit for hours enthralled by Saturday morning television. Of course they sit and watch for long periods: they are effectively in a trance. Television viewing is at best a passive experience. It requires no thought, no imagination and no effort. Quality children's programming can be terrific, but most of what's available is anything but.

Parental control If you feel a TV show has value but are worried about its content, watch it with your children then discuss the issues afterwards.

making rules Television is best doled out carefully in planned and measured doses. Children really do not need television to entertain themselves. Establish some family ground rules that make sense to you. Determine the shows that you are happy for your children to watch, and limit the number of hours a day you allow your children to spend in front of the set. Give your children as much choice as possible: "You can choose from among the following programmes; however, you can only watch three of them in any one day. What do you want today's choices to be?"

Some parents consider whether or not commercial television is appropriate on a case-by-case basis. Sometimes a programme may have real value, but it may have confusing or disturbing content. In these cases, the whole family should watch it and then discuss the issues it raises together once it has finished.

Select videos and DVDs with an educational element, but again limit the amount of time that your children spend watching them.

CHAPTER
FIVE

exploring
the wider
world

KEY
IDEA

children are
little scientists

Children have an inbuilt drive for discovery. Encourage your child to observe the world and to feel a sense of wonder for everything in it.

"see the world as your child sees it – up close and low to the ground"

Maria Montessori believed that all children behave like "little scientists" in that they are eager to observe and make "what if" discoveries about their world. Babies and toddlers test the environment to see what happens when, for example, they drop a toy out of their highchair or play with the water in their bath. This drive for discovery continues to develop as they grow and become more adventurous in the things that they try out, from making mudpies in the garden to starting a worm farm in the living room. Children are born with marvellous imaginations and a keen desire to explore the world. Encourage this in your child – help her to discover the beauty and wonder of everything around her.

child's eye view Remember that your child's world is up close and low to the ground. Seeing life from her point of view can help you to rediscover the sense of wonder of a young child. Keep in mind the slow-moving pace of her world. Follow your child's lead, and be prepared to stop and examine anything that captures her interest – a ladybird or a flower, for example. Don't get impatient when she dawdles – adjust to her pace.

The best way for children to learn is by doing things, not by being told about them. This is especially true when they are young, but it also

applies to older children and even adults. When children are young, they are not only learning things, they are learning how to learn. No book using words and illustrations to describe the world that exists around a small brook or under a rotting log can replace the value of spending time closely studying the real thing. Books and other materials help children to pull these powerful impressions and experiences together in their minds, but the foundation needs to be laid in direct observation and hands-on experience.

the outdoor world
Children love to be outdoors, wandering around, climbing trees, picking berries, collecting conkers. They enjoy helping to look after the family garden or feeding small animals such as ducks, rabbits and chickens. They form lifelong memories of days spent hiking with their parents in the woods, playing in a creek and walking along a beach looking for shells.

You will probably begin your child's life outdoors by taking her out for little excursions in her pushchair or carrying her on your back. Take time to introduce her to your world. Even very young babies absorb the sights and sounds of the outdoors – clouds passing overhead, the sight and

A different perspective Children see the world on a different level from adults. Get down to your child's level and take a look at what she sees.

smell of flowers in the garden, the wind rustling the leaves in the trees. All these leave a strong and lasting impression. Whether it is summer, autumn, spring or winter, every season has its own beauty. Point out small things: a tiny flower poking up through the snow, a beautiful shell, a perfect leaf.

As your child gets older, begin to point out familiar things as you walk around. "Look, there's Grandma's house! What lovely flowers she has growing outside her door!" or "My goodness, Mary, can you see the nest those birds have built in the tree? Some day they will lay eggs, and they will have baby birds up there!" In the winter, when you see animal tracks in the fresh snow, ask "Who has been walking here?"

stewards of the planet

Another key Montessori idea is that children are stewards of the Earth and must learn to care for distant places such as rainforests and ice caps as well as pockets of nature within the city or suburbs, and to preserve them for the future. Teach your child a reverence for life. After all, we are all part of the web of life, dependent on the delicate balance within the natural world for our own existence. For example, children often learn to think of the soil as "dirt", a word that implies something nasty to many people. Teach them to respect good, rich soil and all the life that it supports on our planet.

Emphasize the need to treat every living thing with care. Teach your child not to pick leaves and flowers aimlessly then toss them aside, but to gather them only for a good purpose. It is fine occasionally to gather wild flowers, then dry or press them or place them in a vase with water to preserve them for as long as possible, but never over-pick any one plant or flower. Teach your child to walk gently upon the Earth, taking only what she needs.

Encourage your child to enjoy the forest and meadows, leaving nothing behind. Teach her never to litter. If you see litter on the ground, pick it up and carry it with you until it can be thrown away. This is especially true of bottles, broken glass, cans and plastic bags, which are not only unsightly but also could harm animals. To gather up cans and broken glass safely, you might carry an old canvas shoulder bag. As your child gets older, give her a bag of her own to collect litter in, too.

working in the
family garden

Helping in the garden is a great way to build practical
skills and to feed your child's quest for discovery.

"getting children
to eat vegetables
is rarely a
problem when
they have
grown them
themselves"

When you plan your garden, try to make a space where your child is free
to experiment and grow things. From an early age, children can be involved
in the cycle of the year, from planting seeds indoors or in a cold frame in
the early spring and transplanting the seedlings to the garden when the
danger of frost is past, to tending the garden and watching the fruits and
vegetables grow, all the way to harvest. For young children, there is
something marvellous about going out to the garden and bringing in a
basket of lettuce, spring onions and tomatoes that they helped to grow –
getting children to eat vegetables is rarely a problem when they have
grown, picked and washed them themselves.

Don't forget to include fragrant herbs in your garden. The aroma
of fresh basil, fennel and sage should be part of your child's memories of
childhood. The fact that they can be picked and eaten, adding colour,
scent and flavour to your food, is yet another benefit.

child-sized equipment You can buy garden tools, watering
cans and wheelbarrows that are just the right size for your child. Set up
racks in your garage or garden shed to hold these special tools, and teach
your child to clean them and return them to their places when she is

Budding gardener Teach your child how to plant bulbs and how to look after plants in the garden.

finished for the day. Provide child-sized gardening gloves and sturdy dark green gardening aprons to help teach your child the concept of neatness and order. Look for child-sized baskets to hold the flowers, fruits and vegetables that your child collects as they become ripe and ready to eat.

when space is limited
If you don't have a family garden, consider window boxes or create a container garden. With the right soil, watering and a sunny location, you can raise an amazing amount of produce in a small space – strawberries, tomatoes, peppers, beans and herbs are all easy and convenient to grow. One of the greatest advantages of container gardening is that it puts the garden at a perfect level for small children.

flower power
Leave space in your garden for flowers, both wild flowers native to your region and the traditional annuals and perennials that add beauty to our gardens and grace our tables. Teach your child how to pick them and arrange them in little vases in the house. Young children

often prefer to put one special flower in a very small vase, rather than create large arrangements. You can use the nicely shaped bottles in which individual servings of drinks such as Perrier and Orangina are sold.

Keep your child's flower-arranging kit on a low shelf within her reach. As well as a variety of small containers for her to use, you will also need a small pair of garden scissors to cut the flowers, a small jug to use for adding the water, a funnel to make it easier to pour water into the openings of small vases and a sponge for cleaning up. You might even want to include some small doilies to place under the vases.

Flower arrangements allow your child to bring nature inside your home – they add to the beauty of your rooms, as well as deepening your child's awareness of different plants and flowers.

garden vocabulary

Teach your child the correct names of each flower, fruit and vegetable as they come into season. Before you know it, she will be able to name everything in your garden. You can also teach her the adjectives that describe them: red, large, small, long, rough, silky and so on. Many plants also have practical uses in cooking and around the house. Aloe, as one example, is a wonderful ointment for scrapes and burns.

Hang beautiful pictures of plants and flowers in your home, both close-up art photographs and prints of famous paintings. Your child's library collection should include some of the many wonderful books about flowers, animals and the natural world that have been published. Many children enjoy finding pictures of flowers or leaves they have found in their gardens in the pages of their books.

crafts from nature

Don't forget that all sorts of crafts use flowers, leaves, seeds and grasses. Children love making art with natural materials. They can learn to use a small flower-press to preserve leaves and flowers and mount them in scrapbooks. They can weave with grasses and make little pine-needle baskets. Acorns and pine cones can be used for all sorts of crafts, such as making table decorations; and the branches of many hardwood trees that have pleasing bark can be used to make bark rubbings and nature collages.

animal values

There is no better way to encourage your child to appreciate living things than to invite some to become members of your family. Family pets help to instill compassion and a sense of responsibility. Even a small child can wash a pet's bowl and fill it with food, while older children can be taught how to clean out pens and cages, or take the dog out for walks. If your home allows, consider the possibility of some small farm animals, such as rabbits or chickens, in addition to cats and dogs.

Animals are our fellow travellers on this Earth. Where once people believed that human beings had the right to dominate nature, many of us now understand that we are interdependent with all of the world's plants and animals. More and more people believe that animals deserve kindness and protection from cruelty. Such attitudes begin within your family.

ACTIVITY
FOCUS

going for a walk in
the forest

Make walks in countryside or parkland, exploring
nature, a regular feature of your family life.

You can make walks exciting by adding a goal – set your children the task
of collecting samples of something specific, such as different types of
flowers, leaves, rocks or grasses. Each child can carry a small paper bag for
their specimens. Explain that a specimen is a sample of something that you
find interesting or want to know more about. You may want to put a limit
on how many samples each child may collect (three to five items at most).

When you are out walking be sure to talk to your children about
what they are experiencing. Talk about the weather and the seasons. What
do they notice? What does the sky look like? Is it sunny? Are there clouds?
Point out other things that they might not notice, such as the colours
of leaves on the trees and other seasonal clues. As you walk, encourage
them to remain quiet at times so they can hear the sounds of nature
as well as observing.

Don't be deterred by bad weather – it does children no harm to feel
the sensation of rain or wind on their faces. Children can be expected to
walk a mile for every year of their age, so don't underestimate their
capabilities. Stopping for snacks or a picnic gives them time to recharge as
well as to observe and enjoy the outdoor world around them.

while out and about

follow a squirrel • adopt a tree • roll in the leaves • sit by a lake and watch the geese • look for wild strawberries • hunt for unusual stones • search for wild flowers (don't pick them – observe, study and remember) • lie on your back with your head up against the trunk of a tree and look up into the branches • listen to the wind • watch birds in their nests • follow a butterfly • study the shadows cast by the sun • learn the names of the trees around your home • study the shapes of leaves • use charcoal and tracing paper to make bark rubbings • collect seeds • look for tiny baby trees • search for pine cones • look for animal tracks • find a fallen tree whose wood has begun to decay – explore what lives here • sit still with your eyes closed • listen to the birds calling • look for baby ferns • smell the breezes • find a little glen where fairies might like to live • have a picnic outside in a meadow • run down a hill with your hands spread wide like an aeroplane • float popcorn boats down the stream • pick up litter along the trail • look for mushrooms – but don't eat them!

Learning to observe Take time to stop and examine things your children are attracted to when walking. Don't overburden younger children with too much detail about their discoveries – ask them to describe to you what they can see.

preserving nature

Once you are back home, empty the contents of your specimen bags onto a plastic garden bag and ask your children to tell you what each item is. Is it living or non-living? Where did they find it? What do they know about it? On other occasions, make the weather, birdlife or forest sounds the focus of your walk, and jot down what your children see and hear in a notebook. Explain that if people always collected specimens from nature, eventually there would be nothing left.

LEAFY LESSONS Leaves are a great source of seasonal information. Ask your children to describe their shape and texture as well as colour.

LIVING CREATURES Watching a worm creeping over a leaf will be a source of great interest and entertainment for your little scientist.

LOOK THIS WAY Show your child how to use binoculars to bird watch. Take a spotter book with you to help him identify what he sees.

TALL STORIES Walk at your child's pace, allowing him to stop and absorb what he can see and feel whenever he wants to. Sitting looking up into a tree can provide a different perspective.

make your own
nature museum

When your child brings specimens home, help him to create
his own nature area where he can observe and learn.

nature equipment

These items will be useful for
equipping your nature museum:

- magnifying glass
- microscope
- spotter scope on a tripod
- sound-amplifying microphones
- bug boxes and jars
- terrarium
- ant farm
- aquarium
- bird cage
- cricket cage
- spotter books for identification
- cards for labelling

Most children have a strong desire to bring some samples of nature home
with them and will be delighted if you can find ways to accommodate their
finds. Depending on the space you have available, a nature area in your
child's room can be anything from a simple table of "finds" to an aquarium
and terrarium housing the bugs, beetles, frogs, turtles and other small animals
that he has found and invited back for a short stay.

In our home, we called our nature museum the Dew Drop Inn. In the
spring and early summer we had small flowerpots holding wild flowers
and baby trees that we found in the nearby woods. We brought caterpillars
back to keep in a covered terrarium so that we could see the chrysalids
that formed and the moths or butterflies that emerged. We collected frogs'
eggs and watched them turn into tadpoles before releasing them in the
pond near our house. From time to time, we even hatched baby chicks in
an incubator. And, of course, the occasional litter of kittens or puppies was
always the highlight of any year.

outside inside Our children studied flowers, comparing different
species and counting petals and stamens. In the autumn, they collected
fruits, nuts and berries, noticing how they were distributed and which

Eye spy Oswin takes a closer look through his spotter scope.

animals looked at them as food. They brought specimens back to the nature museum for identification, labelling and display. They also collected and pressed flowers and leaves, mounting them onto cardboard or into bound scrapbooks. On small shelves, the children displayed collections of their finds: abandoned beehives, birds' nests and eggs, snake skins, tree sections and samples of familiar tree wood, cocoons, mounted insects and preserved animal bones.

Tightly covered terrariums and aquariums provided homes for many families of ants, chameleons, newts, lake bass and turtles that came to visit our house for a while. Root boxes – planters with one wall of glass so roots can be seen growing – were a big hit when the children were young.

As your child gets older, he may like to keep a journal of his observations at home and in the field. Encourage him to write poems and stories that capture the sense of wonder and beauty all around him. Older children often enjoy drawing and photographing nature, from sweeping landscapes to an isolated flower or mushroom brought home to the nature shelf.

playing nature-based
party games

There are many great games for parties or groups of children
that teach them about the world. Here are three of them.

Predator and prey The mountain
lion sits quietly, waiting to catch the
antelope in the waterhole game.

When you have large groups of children over for special
occasions such as birthday parties, play games that will teach
them about some aspect of their world while also keeping
them entertained.

the waterhole game

This game is played by eight or more children – you might
want to play in the garden rather than risk getting your carpets
wet! Tell the children that they are going to pretend to be
animals, such as antelope, coming down to the waterhole at
night to drink. One child is a predator, such as a mountain
lion. He sits in the middle of a large circle, surrounded by cups
of water. He is wearing a blindfold and is "armed" with a
spray bottle of water. One by one, the antelope creep up to take a drink:
picking up a cup of water and carrying it back to their seats. The lion cannot
see them and depends on his hearing. If he hears an antelope approach, he
can spring once, shooting a spray of water in the direction of the sound. If a
child is splashed, he or she must leave the group. Once every antelope has
taken a drink or has been "caught", the game is over.

Tag with a difference Children have great fun pretending to be animals in the food chain.

the food chain game

This is a variation of the game of tag, and is designed to teach children the basic concepts of a simple food chain. Choose a food chain with four levels and describe it to the group of children. For example, plants are eaten by grasshoppers, which in turn are eaten by frogs, which in turn are eaten by hawks completing the food chain.

• Divide the children into three groups. In a group of 10, have seven grasshoppers, two frogs and one hawk.

• Give each child who is pretending to be a grasshopper a small plastic bag, which represents the tiny tummy of a grasshopper. Tie a strip of wide brown ribbon on the arm of each grasshopper.

• Give each child who is pretending to be a frog a bigger bag representing the larger tummy of a frog. Tie a strip of wide yellow ribbon on the arm of each frog.

• Give a large plastic bag to the child who is pretending to be a hawk. This represents the still larger tummy of a hawk. Tie a strip of wide green ribbon on the arm of the hawk.

• Now spread a thin layer of popcorn across the carpet or lawn to represent the plant food for the grasshoppers. Explain to the grasshoppers how they "eat" the popcorn by stooping down to pick it up one piece at a time and putting it in their plastic bags. Set the frogs chasing the grasshoppers and if they catch one, they can empty the popcorn from the grasshopper's tummy (plastic bag) into their own tummy and that grasshopper sits out. Set the hawk to chase the frogs and again if he catches one he can empty the contents of the frog's tummy into his own and that frog sits out. After five minutes, see how many grasshoppers and frogs are still in the game and have survived the food chain.

"the food chain game teaches children the basic concepts of a balanced ecosystem"

the web of life game

This is a good rainy day activity that can be played with 10 or more children. You will need a selection of stuffed toy animals or pictures of animals to represent the various animals in the web of life – a bird, a worm, a frog, a turtle, a fish, a bee, a cow and whatever other familiar creatures you wish to include. You will also need pictures of a tree, grass, a flower and the ocean to represent water. In addition, you will need long strands of different coloured string.

Invite everyone to sit down in a large circle. Ask "Who will be the Sun? The Sun sits here in the middle of our circle." The child who sits in the middle wears something yellow to represent the Sun. "Now what plant or animal would you like to be, Jane? Oh, the wolf! Good. Here you take the toy wolf and hold it in your lap." When each child has picked a plant, bird or other animal, take each in turn. "Who needs the Sun? Do birds need the Sun? Yes, they do!" "Who needs water? Do birds need water? Yes. Do dogs need water? Yes, they do!"

As you connect each plant or animal to whatever it needs, run a piece of string between the two. This builds the web of life, which, when you are finished, is very complex and beautiful. "See, we all need one another!"

making cultures
come alive

Introducing our children to different cultures helps cultivate their
sense of wonder and curiosity as well as dispelling prejudice.

Different worlds By making things
that are foreign accessible to our
children, we help them to appreciate
and understand the wider world.

As parents, we can help our children learn to live in peace and harmony
with all people. We can do this by introducing them to different places in
the world, and filling their minds with wonder and fascination for all the
different cultures at an age when they have yet to encounter the kind of
attitudes that breed fear and prejudice.

All of humanity is part of a global family. We share the same needs, and
have more things in common than divide us. The differences among us
stem from our different cultural ways of meeting these same needs. Rather
than fearing those differences, children can come to understand and
appreciate the cultural richness and diversity that defines us. To learn of far
away places, to dream, to imagine, to hope to go there some day has always
allowed children and adults to embrace the whole world and to care about
its well-being. There is no educational objective more important than to
bring our children into full membership of the human family.

cultural studies
To accomplish our goal, we have to make
things that are foreign to children's experience come alive. Perhaps the
easiest way to do this is through world celebrations and contact with
people from other cultures. Montessori schools make use of hands-on

African girl Young children love to dress up in costumes and play with toys from different countries.

experiences and international celebrations drawn from all over the world. We focus our studies on one given theme or topic at a time, looking at it from many perspectives. For example, when we study Africa, we look at the land itself, the climate, the plants and animals that live there, the people and their housing, food, dress, lifestyles, stories and legends, art, music, traditional dance and celebrations. Everything in our approach to a new topic is multi-sensory, hands-on and interconnected.

You can use much the same approach at home. Young children are interested in other children. They like to hear stories about how children live in other countries. They enjoy trying new artwork and listening to music. They love to learn songs and folk dances from around the world. Dressing up in different costumes is fun and creates a lasting impression, especially if accompanied by food, song, dance and a good story. Food in particular lends itself to a sensorial experience and most children will try something new if they are also involved in the process of preparing it.

cultural holidays

As well as celebrating your family's own traditional religious or cultural holidays each year, try finding out about or going to watch some other cultural celebrations. These are often memorable experiences for young children. Here are some of the major holidays:

• Chinese New Year
• Rosh Hashana and Yom Kippur (Jewish)
• Chanukah (Jewish)
• Passover (Jewish)
• Diwali (Hindu)
• Eid (Muslim)
• Christmas (Christian)
• New Year's Day
• Easter (Christian)
• Valentine's Day
• St Patrick's Day
• May Day
• Mother's Day
• Father's Day
• Shrove Tuesday
• Hallowe'en
• Guy Fawkes and bonfire night

which culture?

Start small and simple. Just focus on one country for your first year. You might like to start with a lovely picture book or a video about the country. Simple things such as collecting pictures and postcards are a good early step.

Keep the following points in mind:
• Begin by admitting that you don't know everything about the culture you are studying, but just like your child, you are learning more.
• Convey curiosity and adventure. Pretend that you are going with your children on a trip to this strange country, and you are preparing for it.
• Always speak with respect and care about the culture. Children pick up your underlying emotions.
• Make sure that everything you share with your child about the culture is authentic and accurate.

create a display

Gather as much information as you can about the country you have chosen from your local library and bookstore. Borrow artefacts from relatives and friends who are from the country or who have been there: some people may be willing to loan you artwork, recordings of foreign music or authentic native costumes. These can be displayed in your home for a short time, and then returned.

If you are lucky enough to be visiting the country you are interested in, make a collection while you are there. Look for stamps, coins and paper money; souvenirs; newspapers and magazines; postcards showing cities, famous landmarks and everyday scenes; small examples of typical artwork and crafts, from pottery to baskets, carvings and statuettes to posters, model houses, boats and so forth; dolls dressed in traditional native costume; traditional hats and costumes that the children can try on. If you know someone else who is going, give them a wish list.

Set up a special area, a table or shelf, somewhere in your home to display your treasures: dolls, toys, artwork, books, model houses, picture collections, coins and such like. It is useful to have a wall behind your display so you can hang a poster or painting as part of your display. Your children and their friends should find the cultural display attractive and appealing. Decorate it with items such as paper lanterns, sculpture, brightly imprinted fabrics, flags, ornamental fans and flowers.

Russian dolls Some cultural souvenirs make great sensory activities, too.

a Montessori
birthday party

Montessori schools use a special celebration that you
can easily adopt at home to mark your child's birthday.

The story so far A candle
represents the Sun and a globe
represents Earth. Photos tell the
story of your child's life to date.

Traditional birthday parties often tend to focus on presents, party bags and lots of sugary food. A Montessori birthday celebration takes a different approach, aiming to introduce a little wider understanding and ceremony into the proceedings. Children are given a first impression of the relationship between Earth and the Sun and taught that a year is the amount of time it takes for Earth to circle the Sun once. Children are also told the story of their lives, year by year, from birth to the present day.

counting the years
You will need a small globe to represent Earth, a candle or lamp to represent the Sun, and a circle (or ideally, an ellipse) drawn on the floor with masking tape or laid out with a long piece of yarn, representing the orbit of Earth around the Sun. Make notes about important events in your child's life to date, and collect photos of her at different ages to help tell the story of her life so far.

On the day of your child's birthday, gather your family around the line, leaving plenty of space so the birthday child can walk freely. Bring the candle (or lamp) and the globe to the gathering. Have your notes and the photos ready. Place the candle in the middle of the circle and light it. Remind the children that it is fire and is very hot, so they must sit in their

An annual event Mia's mum lights the candle at the centre of the rope circle and explains how Earth takes a year to travel once around the Sun.

places and watch. Say, "This candle (or light) stands for the Sun – the same Sun that we see up in the sky. The Sun is a great big ball of fire that keeps on burning and doesn't go out."

Take the globe and walk slowly around the line on the floor, saying: "This globe stands for Earth – the planet we live on. Earth goes around the Sun. It takes a long time for Earth to go around the Sun. Every time Earth goes all the way around the Sun, a whole year has gone by. It takes a year for Earth to go around the Sun one time."

Four years old today Mia carries Earth around the Sun four times representing the years of her life so far.

Moving on Mia blows out the candle at the end of the ceremony.

Memory box Mia's collection of mementos of the year are kept in a box so she can look through them.

Now give the globe to the birthday child and ask her to get ready to walk slowly around the line just as you did. Begin to tell her story, something along these lines: "Today is Mia's birthday, and we are going to celebrate it in our special way. Mia is going to carry the globe and walk slowly around the line four times, because she is four years old.

"Mia is just beginning her journey with Earth around the Sun. She hasn't been born yet. Mummy and Daddy are waiting anxiously for her time to come, and Grandma and Grandpa Willis have come to stay at our house to help with the new baby when she is born. Mia, would you take one step forward please?" Mia walks forward one step.

"Now Mia has been born. It is October 28, 2002. She is tiny – only this big – and all pink and wrapped up in a blanket. Mummy and Daddy are so proud. Here is a picture of Mia as a newborn baby.

"Mia, would you walk all the way around the line? Stop when you get back to that spot. Mia is one year old and she is celebrating her first birthday with her family…" Continue the story in this manner. When Mia has walked around the line the correct number of times for her present age, say: "Mia is now four years old, and today is her birthday. Earth has gone around the Sun four times. Four years have gone by since Mia was born."

You may wish to end the celebration by singing a birthday song, then let your child blow out the candle.

Some families like to compile a time capsule of objects to help their children to look back on and remember the year gone by. This might include photos, a copy of a family video, a letter from mum and dad, and perhaps some art or other objects that your child decides to add. The box should be kept where she can look through them whenever she wishes.

Happy days Mia shares photographs of herself at different ages with her friend Ali.

CHAPTER
SIX

the best
time to
learn

the foundations for learning

The sensitive period for language begins at birth and all young children respond to an environment that is rich in words.

pushy parents

Learning is not a race! Children learn at their own pace and, in general, the more parents push, the more children resist. Pushy parents see children as an extension of their own status as adults; if they have a child who reads at three, then clearly they have done their job as parents well. But if a child ends up quietly resentful of lessons, teachers, work books and tests, then what have we really accomplished?

Some children also enter their sensitive period for learning academic skills at an early age, others will not show the slightest interest until they are older. With the right approach you can increase the odds that your child will want to learn to read, write and work with numbers with natural enthusiasm. This chapter shows you how to let your child develop at her own pace, within a home environment that sets a good example and provides the right stimulation and support.

reading aloud Most of us provide a wide variety of books for our young children. Publishers increasingly appreciate the importance of beautifully illustrated children's books, and wonderful selections are available. As my grandmother used to say, "No matter how tight our budget was over the years, we always made money available for good books."

As soon as your baby is able to sit and focus, she will enjoy short periods spent on your lap looking at picture books and hearing you talk about what is on the page. As she grows, read to her every day, not only at bedtime, but whenever you can. Pay attention to her favourites and try to maintain your enthusiasm when you are expected to read them over and over again. Children are absorbing those stories into themselves by repetition.

keep talking

As you care for your baby and toddler, talk about what you are doing. This ties your actions to language, and helps your child to develop an extensive vocabulary. "I am going to change you now. Oh my, were you wet!" or "I am going to pick you up. Here we go. I'm lifting you up high on to my shoulder."

Talk about what you see your child doing as it happens. "You must be very thirsty. You are drinking so much today." "You dug that hole just right for this flower. Now you can put the flower in the hole." Speak clearly and be very specific in what you say: "Put all of the blue buttons in with the other blue buttons." Although your child may not understand what words mean, there is no need to use baby talk.

It is important, however, not to assume that your child understands you. Use simple words and phrases and look her in the eye as you speak to her. If you watch her eyes, you can usually tell if she understands what you are saying or is confused. Does she look away? Demonstrate your meaning if your child does not seem to understand.

Family reading time Reading to your children regularly helps give them a love of books.

Talking together Speak clearly and precisely to your child. Her eyes will tell you whether or not she has understood what you are saying.

As your child's ability to understand grows, the language you use should become more complex in vocabulary and sentence structure. Stretch her with new words. Turn the TV or radio off unless you are watching or listening together – a noisy environment hinders language development.

When your child is very young, help her to communicate without words. Use pantomime to act out stories or situations. Invite your child to play, too. "Pretend that you are carrying a giant puppy, as big as a horse!" "Pretend that you are a bird flying in the sky. Flap your wings like this!" You can also act out what many words mean (big, tall, fast, slow, smile, sad). Older children continue to enjoy this, too.

teaching household names
Teach your child the correct names for things around the house. In their sensitive period for language, children can easily absorb new words and grasp their meaning.

The more words they learn, the better! Even though your child may make words up or mispronounce them, don't use silly words yourself. Just use the correct name, recognizing that your child's ability to understand and vocalize a complete range of sounds will develop in stages. For example, in the first instance your child learns the word "dog", and learns to distinguish a dog from a cat. From there, you can begin to teach words that further define dogs and cats. Learning that your dog "Biscuit" is a French poodle, and your neighbour's dog "Toby" is a Bassett hound would be one example.

Learning the names of familiar animals and birds found around your neighbourhood, flowers and trees, fruits, vegetables, body parts and things found around your home are all good examples that can be taught using the Montessori three-stage lesson (see pages 166–7). A large vocabulary is a solid foundation for a lifetime of learning.

using descriptive words
Once your child knows the words for lots of objects, start to extend her vocabulary by teaching her words that describe the objects and their location. You can start with words that describe the colours of objects. First, introduce primary colours (red, blue and yellow), then secondary colours (green, orange, purple, brown and so on), and then familiar shades of colours (lilac, rose, pastel blue, tan and so on). You can then teach her words that describe colours, such as pale blue, deep pink, bright yellow. You can also introduce your child to words that describe size (big or small, short or tall, thin or wide), taste (salty, sweet, bitter, sour), weight (light and heavy), texture (rough and smooth) and so on.

As your child learns the basic descriptive adjectives, begin to introduce her to comparative language: bigger and biggest, longer and longest, taller and tallest. This vocabulary is essential when children are working with the sensory activities described in chapter two. "Which one of these cubes is the largest? Now, which one comes next?"

Once your child has a good grasp of descriptive words, ask her to describe things in her own words. "How would you describe Toby (your neighbour's Bassett hound)?" Encourage her to retell stories or to describe what she is doing as you make dinner together.

the command game

It may not seem to be the case sometimes, but children love to follow orders in a game. Start with simple one-step commands: "Please give me the toy truck" or "Please give me the truck that is over there." Then make commands more challenging by adding a description of an object and its location. "Would you give me the large red bucket on the top shelf over there?" For young children this gets much more difficult if the object you ask for is in another room. Don't be surprised if they get lost along the way if you try this too soon.

The game can be made more challenging as children get older by adding in more than one step. "Would you please take these flowers to the work top next to the sink and put them down? Then choose a vase and put about this much water in it. Then put the flowers in the vase and arrange them to make them pretty for the table. When you are finished, put them on the table and we will make it very special for our guests."

enriching vocabulary

Montessori teachers use a three-stage process to help children develop a rich vocabulary. Children learn what words mean when they can associate the name with an object. For example, here's how you might teach a young child the names of secondary colours.

In the first step show your child an orange-coloured paint sample. Name the colour: "This is orange." Now show your child a green-coloured paint sample. Name its colour: "This is green." Finally, show your child a purple-coloured paint sample and say, "This is purple."

In the second step, you help your child make a link between the language and his own experience by giving him the name of an object and asking him to find it. "Show me orange." He should point to the orange sample. Next ask him to "show me purple" and he should point to the purple sample. If your child makes a mistake, simply re-teach the lesson. Returning to the first step, point to the purple sample and restate, "This is purple." Point to the green sample and restate, "This is green."

In the third step, we ask children to name something without naming it first as we did before. Point to one of the paint sample and ask, "What colour is this?" Your child should answer, "Orange." If he makes a mistake, re-teach the lesson by patiently reconfirming the names of the objects, using the first and second steps.

a broad range of words To begin with you can use the three-stage lesson approach to introduce your child to lots of different everyday objects, such as types of fruit or vegetables (for example, pepper, artichoke and butternut squash, as shown on the facing page), animals, birds and household objects. Repeat the game with the same set of objects over several days or weeks – only move on to a new set of objects when your child is ready.

As your child gets older you can continue to enrich his vocabulary by using the three-stage lesson. Introduce terms from geometry (equilateral triangle, square, cube, pentagon), botany (plant, grass, tree, leaf, stem, lower, petal, stamen) or the various land and water forms that make up our planet's surface (island, lake, ocean, river, isthmus). The more words children know, the more they observe and try to identify what's around them.

step by step: the three-stage lesson

ONE Oswin's mum tells him the names of three different vegetables. She points to each one as she says its name.

TWO Now she asks him to point to one of them – the butternut squash. She does this for each vegetable in turn.

THREE His mum then picks up one of the vegetables and asks Oswin what its name is.

Story time Ask your child to choose a picture she likes, then to tell you a story about it. This helps develop her vocabulary and story-telling skills.

Robin redbreast Cherry chooses a picture of a robin. She cuts it out, then glues it onto a clean sheet of paper.

Tell me a tale Cherry makes up her story about the robin and her mum writes it down as she tells it.

telling a story Ask your child to choose an interesting picture in a magazine and to cut it out. Then ask her to tell you something about the characters or animals shown in the picture. Your older child may want to make up a story. Write down what she says, word for word, printing it out neatly, or type it into the computer and print it out using a large font. If you print just one sentence per page, with the text at the bottom, your child may like to glue in her picture, then add her own illustrations for the different pages. Print them on nice paper and bind them into a book by punching holes in the paper and tying a ribbon through each hole.

Help your child sign her name on her work when she has finished. If she can't write yet, encourage her to make a mark or to write out one letter. She will begin to sense the connection between marks written on paper and the spoken word.

"when your child is ready to talk, be ready to listen; you can prompt her by asking what she thinks will happen next in a story"

questions and feelings When your child is ready to talk, be ready to listen. At other times, prompt her by, for example, asking what she thinks will happen next in a story. "How did the baby bear know someone had been sitting in his chair?" "It was broken and someone big must have sat in it." Open-ended questions help your child to develop her ability to organize and communicate her thoughts out loud. "What would you see if you were a bird flying high up in the sky over our house?" "What could happen if…?"

Encourage your child to talk about her feelings. Prepare a set of photos cut from magazines that show people experiencing different emotions – happy, sad, angry, frightened, joyful. Ask her which emotions are shown in the pictures, then ask her to talk about her own feelings. "What happens when you feel scared?"

the writing road
to reading

The process of learning how to read can be as simple
and painless as the process of learning how to speak.

presenting **letters**

Present letters to your child a
few at a time, in these groups:

first set	c m a t
second set	s r i p
third set	b f o g
fourth set	h j u l
fifth set	d w e n
sixth set	k q v x y z

In Montessori schools we use a hands-on phonetic approach that helps young children to form a clear understanding of how written words encode the spoken sounds of our language into the symbolic letters of the alphabet. Using this technique, children master the sounds made by each letter, as well as the letter represented by each sound, one letter at a time until the entire alphabet has been mastered. With some basic equipment you can use the same approach at home.

sandpaper letters These provide a tactile as well as visual way to help children to learn the alphabet. Sandpaper letters are a set of 26 tablets made of painted thin masonite board. On each tablet, a lower case letter has been cut out of fine sandpaper and glued down against a smooth, coloured background. Consonants are printed against pink or red and vowels against blue backgrounds to help children distinguish between them. Sandpaper letters can be bought from a number of suppliers (see page 188) or you can make your own (see box on facing page).

As soon as your child shows interest, typically around age three, introduce her to a few letters at a time (see box left). Show her how to trace each letter as it would be written, using the middle and index fingers

how to make sandpaper letters

Use thin masonite board or sturdy cardboard to prepare 26 tablets 20cm (8in) high by 15cm (6in) wide. Some letters, such as "w" may need a wider tablet. Using a non-toxic spray enamel paint, paint each of the tablets. Use blue paint for the tablets for the vowels – a, e, i, o and u – and pink or red for the tablets for the consonants – b, c, d, f, g, h, j, k, l, m, n, p, q, r, s, t, v, w, x, y, z.

Next, you need to cut out your letters from fine sandpaper. We have prepared files with the letters made quite large, which you can download from our website (there is a file for lower case letters at www.montessori.org/sitefiles/ alphabet_low.pdf and another for capital letters at www.montessori. org/sitefiles/alphabet_caps.pdf). Print them out then use a razor knife to cut out each of the letters to make a stencil that you can then use to cut out your 26 sandpaper letters. Glue each letter down onto a tablet, sandpaper side up.

of the hand she normally uses to hold things. As you demonstrate, say the sound that the letter represents in a three-letter phonetic word, such as "cat". The letter "c", for example, represents the sound "kuh".

Sit down beside your child with two sandpaper letters on a small rug. We'll use the letter "c", pronounced "kuh", and the letter "m", pronounced "mmm". While tracing the letter "c" say "This is 'kuh'. Can you say 'kuh'?" Most children will then say it after you. Now invite your child to trace and sound the letter. As she traces its shape, she is receiving three distinct impressions: the shape of the letter, the feel of its shape and how it is written, and the way you pronounce its sound. Now think up words that begin with this sound: "Kuh, cat, can, cap…" This is the first stage of a three-stage lesson (see pages 166–7). At this point, introduce the second letter, using the same process. Continue on to the second stage of the lesson. "Can you show me 'kuh'? Can you show me 'mmm'?" If your child makes a mistake, represent the first stage again. "This is 'kuh'. This is 'mmm'." Then try the second stage again. "Can you show me 'mmm'? Can you show me 'kuh'?" Now go to the third lesson. Lay out the tablets for the letters "c", "a" and "t" before your child and she will pronounce each in turn, "kuh", "aah", "tuh": "cat". She has just read her first word!

Gradually introduce more letters, perhaps two more each week or so, until your child has mastered the entire alphabet. Remember to follow your child. If she becomes bored, end the lesson – your goal is to instill a love of learning and real interest in reading and composing words, not to produce an early reader at any cost.

Many parents find it curious that in Montessori schools children are not taught the names of the letters, but the sounds that we pronounce as we phonetically sound out words one letter at a time. For a long time, they may not know the names of letters at all, but will call them by the sounds they make "buh", "cuh", "aah" and so on. This eliminates one of the most unnecessary and confusing steps that most children have to go through in learning to read: "A stands for apple. The sound it makes is 'aah'."

It is not uncommon to find that young children who are learning to read this way will be able to compose simple words using prepared alphabet letters several weeks or months before they will be able to read them comfortably. This is a by-product of Montessori's carefully planned introduction to language. Rather than learning words by sight, children spell phonetic words out one sound at a time, which is easier than the process of "decoding" printed words into their component sounds.

Letters in sand Once your child has learnt to trace letters on paper, she can try tracing them in a tray of sand.

tracing letters in fine sand
A nice extension of the sandpaper letters is to invite your child to trace the letters that she is learning in fine sand, in a tray that is deep enough to minimize accidental

spills. After tracing a sandpaper letter on paper, ask her to trace it in the sand. This reinforces her muscular memory of the process of forming the letter and helps her eventual transition into handwriting.

developing pencil control

Your child needs to develop control of her hand before she can begin to learn to write. Many of the sensorial activities that we have covered in earlier chapters have the extra advantage that they help your child begin to develop the hand-eye coordination so important for handwriting. Give her good-quality coloured pencils to colour shapes on good-quality paper as a step towards handwriting. Show her how to shade in the shapes carefully using parallel strokes.

A small chalk board and chalk are useful when your child is ready to write. Have her trace one of the sandpaper letters with her fingers, and then try to write it on the chalk board. When she can write individual letters, challenge her to begin to compose simple words.

Writing with chalk Give your child a chalk board on which to practise writing letters with chalk.

playing with letters

This game reinforces children's mastery of the sounds of the letters they are learning, as well as helping them to recognize the first sound in any word. To play, you will need to gather five small objects whose names begin with the same letter. For example, for the letter "t" you might use a toy train, a truck and a tractor. Place two or three sandpaper letters on a mat. Place the objects in a basket. Ask your child to select one of the objects and name it. Then ask her, "What sound do you hear at the beginning of the word 'truck'." Pronounce it carefully, sound by sound: "tuh" "rrr" "uhh" "kuh". "Truck begins with 'tuh'. Let's put the truck below the 'tuh' over here." Your child should continue until all of the objects have been placed.

the movable alphabet

Once your child has begun to recognize several letters and their sounds with the sandpaper letters, you can introduce her to a movable alphabet. This is a large box with compartments containing plastic letters, organized much like an old-fashioned printer's box of metal type. You can buy Montessori movable alphabets (see page 188) or you can substitute various other forms of plastic or magnetic letters made for children. Your child can compose

Movable alphabet A large box with
26 compartments holds plastic letters
which children use to spell out words.

words by selecting a small object or picture and then laying out the word with the movable letters. As with the sandpaper letters, she sounds out words one letter at a time, selecting the letter that makes the next sound.

This phonetic approach has long been recognized by educators as the single most effective way to teach children how to read and write. However, we have to remember that, unlike Italian and Spanish, English is not a completely phonetic language. Just consider the several different sounds made by the letters "ough". There is the sound "off" as in "cough", or "uff" as in "rough" or "enough", or the sound "ohhh" as in the word "though", or the sound "ott" as in "thought". Altogether, there are some 96 different phonograms (combinations of letters that form distinct sounds) in the English language (such as "ph-", "-ee", "ai", "oo" and so on).

As your child begins to compose words, phrases, sentences and stories, her spelling may sometimes get a bit creative. For example, she may spell the word phone as "fon". Don't worry about correcting her spelling during these early days – it is much better to encourage her to become more confident in her ability to sound words out, rather than risking her losing interest because she gets it wrong.

The process of composing words with the movable alphabet continues for many years, gradually moving from three-letter words to four- and five-letter words with consonant blends ("fl", "tr", "st"), double vowels ("oo", "ee"), silent "e"s and so on.

starting to read

Typically, there is a smooth transition from reading and writing single words to sentences and stories. For some children this will happen at age four, for others when they are five or six. A few will read earlier, others will take longer. But all children are different and it is useless to fret if your child isn't as eager as her contemporaries.

No matter how young, as soon as your child shows the slightest interest, begin to teach her how to read. When she is ready, she will pull it all together and will begin to read and write on her own. Use your computer to make cards printed with the names of familiar objects on them. Your child can practise reading these as she uses them to label all sorts of objects around your home.

the verb game

When your child can read whole words, try a more sophisticated version of the command game. Make a set of cards, on each of which is printed a single one-word command (a verb).

Your child picks a card, reads it, then asks you to hold it up while she performs the command: hop, smile, yawn, sleep, clap, sit, stand, wave, eat, drink, put her hands on her head and so on.

Once she can read one-word command cards, create more advanced card sets using complete sentences: "Bring me a doll" or "Waddle across the room like a duck."

first steps to
mathematics

Teach your child simple maths concepts using
games and hands-on learning materials.

Learning to count by rote is the easiest activity to build into your daily life.
You can count with your child in many situations: when cooking together,
count how many spoonfuls you need to add; when out walking, count
steps from one to 10, then start again. A simple game involves gently
tossing a bean bag back and forth between you and your child, counting
every time it's thrown. Continue as high as your child knows, then keep
going yourself once your child is no longer certain.

what numbers mean Grasping the concept of numbers by
counting separate objects is more difficult at first. While young children
can learn to "count" by rote, reciting the sequence of numbers from one
to 10, most cannot easily grasp the difference between one quantity and
another when looking at more than three or four objects. It's almost as if
they are thinking: "One, two, three… many!"

One way to avoid this is by allowing children to visualize the concepts
of numbers and quantity by using a series of segmented rods, rather than
trying to teach them to count sets of separate objects. In Montessori
classrooms, we use a set of rods that vary in length by 10cm (4in). The

One, two, three Counting is a
fundamental mathematical skill.

making
number rods

To make your own set of number rods, use wooden lathe or strip board, approximately the same dimensions as many rulers (5cm/2in wide by about 1cm/½in high). You need to cut or have someone cut 10 lengths: 10cm (4in) long, 20cm (8in), 30cm (12in), through 100cm (40in). Spray paint the entire set of strips red and allow them to dry.

Then, using masking tape, carefully mark off the parts that should be painted blue. For example, the "one" rod is all red. The "two" rod is red for the first 10cm (4in), then blue for the next 10cm (4in). The "three" rod is red for the first 4in (10cm), blue for the next 4in (10cm), then red again for the last 4in (10cm). This creates an alternative length of red, blue, red sections. Continue through to the "10" rod, which should be 100cm (40in) in length, painted red, blue, red to form 10 alternating sections.

Steps to numbers To introduce number rods, show your child how to arrange them into a stair from largest to smallest. Count each coloured segment together.

shortest rod is 10cm (4in) long and is painted red. The second is 20cm (8in) long, and is divided into two 10cm (4in) segments, one red and one blue. This continues through all 10 rods. You can buy the Montessori number rods (see page 188) or make your own (see panel).

One of the insights children begin to get from working with the rods is the nature of addition and the concept that two numbers can add to each other. For example, when the children place the "one" number rod at the end of the "two" rod, they create a new rod that is the same length as the "three" rod just above. They explore similar relationships with all of the numbers from one to 10.

IN THE BASKET As he throws bean bags into a basket, Max calls out the number he gets on target.

POTATO COUNTING Holly practises counting with all sorts of household items.

FIRST MATHS Oswin counts oranges in a bowl. His mum removes two and asks "How many are there now?"

counting baskets These baskets help young children to make the next step in coming to understand the concepts of number and quantity. You need a set of 10 small baskets, each with a card attached labelling the baskets 0, 1, 2, 3, up to 9. You will also need a larger basket containing 45 identical pieces. In Montessori schools we use wooden dowels 1cm (½in) in diameter and 15cm (6in) in length, but at home you could use large wooden beads of the same colour or clothespegs. Show your child how to count out the correct number of pieces to go in each basket: one, two, three, all the way to nine. Naturally, the basket labelled "0" is left empty, teaching your child at an early age the concept that zero means none (an empty set). If your child counts correctly there will not be any pieces left over when the compartment labelled "9" is filled up.

simple sums There are all sorts of things you can do with your child around the house to help her practise her skills. Try using dolls to illustrate simple sums: "When Mummy and Daddy first got married there were two of them. Then baby is born. How many are there now?" You can do the same with pieces of fruit or anything else that comes to hand.

exploring science in your home

Your home is an ideal place for scientific experiments that help your child discover how the world works.

Magical magnetism Investigating the magnetic properties of different objects is a favourite science activity.

There are so many science activities you can do with your child that I could fill an entire book with them. Many of the activities I have already suggested in this and earlier chapters are science-related: sensory awareness exercises, nature walks, working together in the garden and the like. Here are just a few more ideas to get your young scientist started.

magnetic or non-magnetic

Place a number of small objects in a basket, making sure that some of them are made of ferrous material (iron) and can be picked up with a magnet. Prepare two cards, one reading "Magnetic" and the other "Non-magnetic". Ask your child to use a small magnet to see which objects it will pick up and which it will not, then place the objects alongside the correct card.

living or non-living

Fill a basket with toys and small novelty store objects that represent things that are alive (organic) and non-living (inorganic). Prepare cards labelled "Living" and "Non-living". For the objects representing living things you might choose toy birds, forest animals, insects, a tree and people. For the non-living objects, you might choose objects such as a magnet, a thimble, a toy car, a model house and a small mirror. Ask your child to set the things that would be living and non-living in the real world alongside the appropriate card.

sink or float

Gather a number of objects, some of which you know will float and others which will sink. Invite your child to predict which objects will sink and which will float. Set up a basin of water on a tray and place the objects in the water so he can see if he is right.

sprouting seeds

For this experiment, you will need dried, uncooked butter beans, paper towels and a

plant mister. Show your child how to take a butter bean, place it on a paper towel, wrap it up gently and then spray the seed and paper towel with water from the plant mister. Remind him to spray the paper towel every day to keep the seed damp. Check for signs that it is starting to sprout. When it does, show your child how to transplant it into a small flowerpot filled with potting soil. Remind him to keep it moist.

Floating fun and games Your child will love to test whether or not objects float or sink in a large bowl of water.

a basket of living grass

Take a small basket and fill the bottom with plastic film. Help your child to add 2cm (1in) of small pebbles, then 5cm (2in) of potting soil. Show him how to sprinkle grass seeds over the potting soil and gently press them in. Place the basket on a table next to a window and remind your child to use a plant mister several times a day to keep the seeds damp. In about two weeks he will see the grass seed begin to germinate.

grow a sock

In autumn, our socks and trousers tend to pick up burrs and other clinging seeds when we go for walks in the woods or through tall grass. Give your child a pair of long sports socks to put on over his trouser legs. Go for a

Making sail boats Use walnut shells, cardboard, toothpicks and modelling clay to make sail boats that can be launched on a man-made lake.

walk through areas where you are certain to encounter these hitchhiking seeds. When you get home, place the socks in a basin in a place where they will get lots of sun. Soak the socks, leaving one end in the water to continue to soak up more moisture like a wick. After a week or two, the seeds will begin to germinate and your child will have "grown a living sock"!

exploring roots

Gently dig up a plant with its roots intact. Place it on newspaper and carefully pull the soil away to expose the roots. Explain to your child that every plant uses its roots to absorb water and nutrients from the soil. Repack the soil around the roots and replace the plant in the soil.

walnut shell sailboats

Children love playing in water. Use a deep tray filled with water as a little lake on which your children can sail small boats made from walnut shells. To make the boats, open a few walnut shells along the edges, being careful

not to damage the half shells. Then show your children how to make a sail from a piece of sturdy cardboard cut to form either a square or a triangle. They can use a toothpick for the mast and mount the sail by poking the toothpick through the cardboard at the right points so that it can catch a breeze. Put modelling clay in the bottom of the shell and put the mast into it to hold it upright. Your children can now launch their boats and gently blow to create a breeze.

pouring air

Young children find it funny that they can make bubbles by submerging a container filled with air underwater and then release (pour) the air by gently tipping the container upwards. This works best in a deep container, such as a bucket, and is even better when the sides of the container are made of glass, like in an aquarium, so everyone can see the bubbles coming up to the surface. At bathtime, your children can have fun blowing bubbles underwater using straws.

is Montessori right for your child?

If you have enjoyed using the ideas in this book at home, you may want to look to a Montessori school for continuing your child's education.

Dance for joy Learning in a Montessori school is a fun, joyful and exciting experience.

One of the strengths of Montessori is the atmosphere of cooperation and respect, as different children find joy in learning. Usually, the method is "right" for a wide spectrum of personalities, temperaments and learning styles. It works for families with a range of learning expectations and, in most cases, parents and teachers work together between home and school to help children learn and develop.

The programme is carefully structured to provide optimal learning opportunities for children. However, parents who are particularly concerned about high achievement may find the Montessori approach difficult to understand and support. While we all want the best for our children, it represents an alternative way from the more conventional thinking found in most schools. The belief is that children are born intelligent, curious and creative, and that all too often schools (and some parents) make the process of learning stressful rather than natural.

Families who are generally rather chaotic and disorganized (arrive late in the morning, pick up children at varying times and find it difficult to attend meetings and work closely with a school) may find a Montessori experience rather frustrating, although the children from such families often cling to this structure and find it very reassuring.

choosing a school

Although most schools try to remain faithful to their understanding of Maria Montessori's insights and research, they have all been influenced by the evolution of our culture and technology over the 100 years since the first Montessori schools were developed. What is more, although the name Montessori refers to a method and philosophy, it is not protected by copyright nor a central licensing or franchising programme. What this means is that, in many parts of the world, anyone could, in theory, open a school and call it Montessori with no knowledge of how an authentic programme is organized or run. When this happens it is both disturbing and embarrassing for those of us who know the difference. Many of these schools fail but often not before they harm the public's perception of the integrity and effectiveness of Montessori as a whole.

Often, one sign of a school's commitment to excellence is its membership in one of the professional Montessori organizations (see page 188). These organizations offer schools the opportunity to become accredited as well. There are many other smaller Montessori organizations, too, but the key is to remember that there is no requirement that a Montessori school be affiliated or accredited by any outside organization. Quite a few Montessori schools choose to remain independent.

The most important question when selecting a Montessori school is to consider how well it matches your sense of what kind of education you want for your children. No single educational approach will be right for all children. Ideally, parents should seek out the best fit, not only between their child and a particular school, but also between their family's values and goals for their children's education and what given schools realistically offer. Finding the right school for parents is as important as finding the right school for a child. There must be a partnership based on the mutual sense that each is a good match for the other.

In determining which school is the best match for all concerned, you need to trust your eyes, ears and gut instincts. Nothing beats your own observation and experience. The school that receives rave reviews from one parent may be completely wrong for another; however, it might be a perfect match for your family. Trust your own experience rather than that of other parents.

Montessori way

Parents who are comfortable with Montessori tend to agree with the following basic ideas about children's learning:

• **Intelligence is not rare** among human beings. It is found in children at birth. With the right stimulation, the development of reasoning and problem-solving skills can be nurtured in young children.

• **The most important years** of a child's education are the first six years of life.

• **Children need to develop** a high degree of independence and autonomy.

• **Academic competition** and accountability are not effective ways to motivate students to become well educated. They learn more effectively when school is seen as a safe, exciting and joyful experience.

• **There is a direct link** between children's sense of self-worth, empowerment and self-mastery, and their ability to learn and retain new skills and information.

• **Children learn best** through hands-on experience, real-world application and problem solving.

In the end, the selection of a Montessori school comes down to a matter of personal preference. If you visit a school and find yourself in love with the look and feel of it and if you can clearly see your child happy and successful in that atmosphere, then that school is more likely to be a good fit than one that leaves you feeling confused and uncertain.

what to look for

As tempting as it is to enrol your child in a school without entering a classroom, put this visit at the top of your "to do" list. You will learn a great deal by spending 30 minutes to an hour watching the children at work. Ask permission to watch a "work period" first. If you have time, stay for a group meeting or come back later to watch this part of the children's day.

• You should not find rows of desks in a Montessori classroom. There will be no teacher's desk and chalk board in the front of the room. The environment will be set up to make it easy for children to talk to each other and work together. The furniture in the classroom will be the right size for the students.

• Classrooms should be bright, warm and inviting, filled with plants, animals, art, music and books. Interest centres will be filled with intriguing learning materials, mathematical models, maps, charts, international and historical artefacts, a class library, an art area, a small natural science museum and animals that the children are raising. In an elementary class, you will also find computers and scientific apparatus.

• Classrooms will be organized into several curriculum areas, usually including: language arts (reading, literature, grammar, creative writing, spelling and handwriting); mathematics and geometry; everyday living skills; sensory awareness exercises and puzzles; geography, history, science, art, music and movement. Each area will be made up of one or more shelf units, cabinets and display tables with a wide variety of materials on open display, ready for use as the children select them.

• Each class should contain the full complement of Montessori materials considered appropriate for that level.

• There will be few if any toys in a Montessori preschool classroom. Instead, there will be an extensive collection of learning materials that match the developmental capabilities, interests and needs of the children

The road to reading In Montessori schools, children learn to read at their own pace when they are ready.

Skilful handling Practising everyday skills, such as spooning, children develop hand-eye coordination.

Nice manners Montessori children are renowned and respected for their courtesy and kindness.

enrolled in each class. These allow for multiple methods of learning and discovery, offering a wide range of intellectual challenges.

• Each class should be led by a Montessori-certified teacher who holds a recognized Montessori credential for the age level taught. In addition, each class would usually include either a second certified Montessori teacher or a para-professional teacher's assistant. You can expect to find teachers working with one or two children at a time, advising, presenting a new lesson or quietly observing the class at work.

• A Montessori programme is composed of mixed age groups of children within each classroom, traditionally covering a three-year span from the early childhood level onwards. Ideally, a Montessori class is balanced in terms of boys and girls as well as in the number of children in each age group. Classes should be made up of 25 to 30 children, although these numbers will be lower at the baby and toddler levels.

• Students will usually be found scattered around the classroom, working alone or with one or two others.

• It should be clear that the children feel comfortable and safe.

addresses and websites

Montessori organizations

Montessori Society AMI (UK)
26 Lyndhurst Gardens
London NW3 5NW
Tel: 020 7435 3646
www.montessori-uk.org
Teacher training and list of accredited schools.

Montessori Centre Internationale (MCI)
18 Balderton Street
London W1K 6TG
Tel: 020 7493 0165
www.montessori.uk.com
Teacher training college.

Montessori Education UK
Tel: 020 8946 4433
www.montessorieducationuk.org
Umbrella organization listing accredited schools.

Montessori St Nicholas Charity
24 Princes Gate
London SW7 1PT
Tel: 020 7584 9987
www.montessori.org.uk
Charity with magazine for parents.

The Montessori Foundation
The International Montessori
Council (IMC)
PO Box 130
2400 Miguel Bay Drive
Terra Ceia Island
Florida 34250
USA
Tel: 00-1-941-729-9565
www.montessori.org
Non-profit educational organization that supports the development of Montessori schools around the world. It also publishes a parents' journal.

manufacturers and suppliers

Michael Olaf Montessori
www.michaelolaf.net
Leading source of Montessori-inspired and compatible educational toys, games, art materials, music and more.

Artful Dodgers
www.artfuldodgers.co.uk

Sense Toys
www.sensetoys.co.uk

Absorbent Minds Montessori
www.absorbentminds.co.uk

Nienhuis Montessori
www.nienhuis.nl

further reading

Britton, Lesley (1992) *Montessori Play and Learn: A Parent's Guide to Purposeful Play from Two to Six* Crown Publishers

Epstein, Paul; Seldin, Tim (2003) *The Montessori Way: An Education for Life* The Montessori Foundation

Gettman, David (1988) *Basic Montessori: Learning Activities for Under-fives* New York: St Martin's Press

Kramer, Rita (1988) *Maria Montessori: A Biography. 2nd ed.* Reading, MA: Addison-Wesley

Lawrence, Lynne (1998) *Montessori Read and Write: A Parent's Guide to Literacy for Children* Three Rivers Press

Montanaro, Silvana (1991) *Understanding the Human Being: The Importance of the First Three Years of Life* Mountain View, CA: Nienhuis Montessori USA

Montessori, Maria (1936) *The Secret of Childhood: A Book For All Parents and Teachers* 1998, London & Hyderbad: Sangam Books (Carter translation)

Montessori, Maria (1948) *The Discovery of the Child* Revised and enlarged edition of *The Montessori Method* (1912). 1988, Oxford: Clio (Trans. M. Joseph Costelloe, based on 6th Italian ed)

Montessori, Maria (1948) *What You Should Know About Your Child.* The following editions are currently in print: 1961, Adyar, Madras, India: Kalakshetra; 1989, Oxford, England: Clio Press

Montessori, Maria (1949) *The Absorbent Mind.* The following editions are currently in print: 1959, Thiruvanmiyur, Madras, India: Kalakshetra (First publication of edition rewritten by Montessori in Italian and translated by Claude Claremont. All subsequent English editions based on this one); 1988, Oxford, England: Clio Press Ltd; 1993, Cutchogue, NY: Buccaneer Books, Inc. (An imprint of Random House); 1995, New York: Henry Holt & Co. (with intro by John Chattin–McNichols)

Polk Lillard, Paula; Lillard Jensen, Lynn (2003) *Montessori from the Start: The Child at Home, from Birth to Age Three* Random House

Seldin, Tim; Epstein, Paul (2003) *The Montessori Way: An Education for Life* The Montessori Foundation

Wolf, Aline (1980) *A Parents' Guide to the Montessori Classroom* Altoona, PA: Parent Child Press

Wolf, Aline (1984) *Mommy, It's a Renoir!* Altoona, PA: Parent Child Press

Wolf, Aline (1989) *Peaceful Children, Peaceful World* Altoona, PA: Parent Child Press

index